Lily Poetry Review

EDITOR-IN-CHIEF

Eileen Cleary

CONTRIBUTING EDITORS

Christine Jones

Lisa Sullivan

FLASH FICTION EDITORS

Mark Jednaszewski

Kody Martin

Sarah Walker

GRAPHIC DESIGN

Martha McCollough

ART EDITOR

Pamela Gemme

MEDIA AND EVENTS

Rebecca Connors

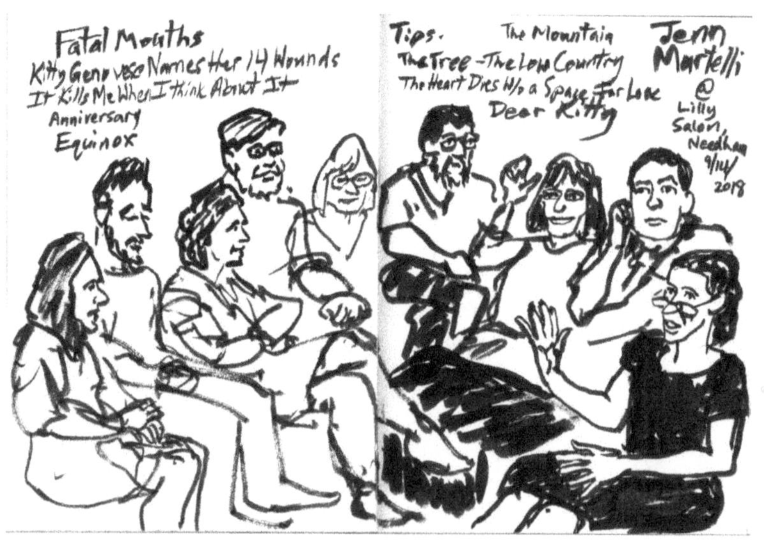

A Letter from the Editor

Dear Readers,

It's a joy to bring you this inaugural Lily Poetry Review, filled with beautiful art and writing. This would not be possible without submitters. Thanks to all of you who shared your pieces with us. It was an honor to consider them, whether or not they were right for this issue.

Whether you hold this journal as a contributor or reader, I hope you will find a writer or an artist to admire here. Maybe you'll adore the beautiful sounds and haunting imagery of Konner Jebb's, "Your Dad's Death Everywhere." Or, you will be taken with the subtext in Kathy Nilsson's brilliant "Incontinent Nostalgia," in which, "The sun set without riffling a child's hair." Perhaps you'll be smitten with Sarah Kirstine Lain's work, which narrows the abyss between artificial intelligence and human perception. If you love a piece of work you see here, please share it with the world, and especially let the author or artist know. Feel free to post on our Facebook page, or message through our website. I'll be sure to pass any comments onto the writers and artists.

Speaking of sharing in joy, this drawing by Peter Urkowitz is of The Lily Poetry Salon, where a group of writers meets to promote, share and support the work of other writers. Urkowitz captures many local readings in his sketches, and it's one fantastic way in which he uses his art to help other artists.

Now, I leave you to your reading.

With Appreciation,

Eileen Cleary

CONTENTS

LAURE-ANNE BOSSELAAR

LAST DAYS IN MAY

Long days alone.
Days lucid & still like this glass of water,
sunlit, on the windowsill.

No one comes to the door except for the mailman's
hurried steps at noon. Catalogs. Charities & bills.
Give to the poor. Pay for the gas.
For that water in your glass.

> Perhaps it's because of this sky, Delft blue, & in its heart
> a sun so mellow it won't beat on anything,
> > or because of the swallows: they're back
> > at last, to shriek, swirl, then nest under the eaves,

> but today, all day, loneliness — this ache, this deep
> lake rippled by longing — drained at last
> > & yielded to a solitude
> > come to nestle here.

How ripe this afternoon! How willingly I'll watch it
die inside the tree. So soon.

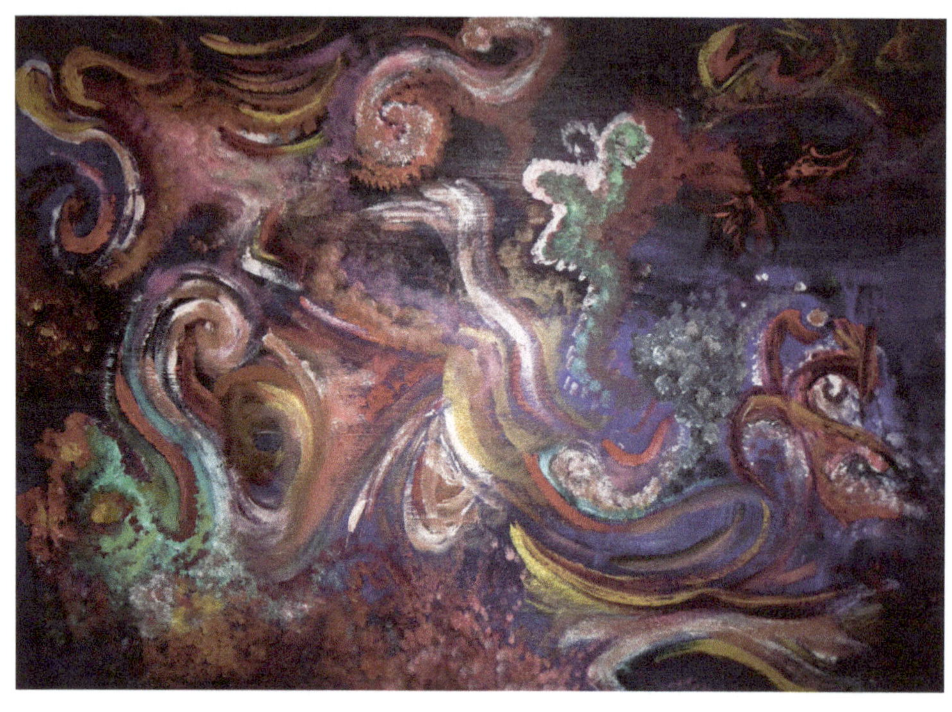

BRENDA BLIGHT
THE DANCE OF DRAGONS IN THIS CELESTIAL SEA

SHEILA BLACK

We Climb More Deeply Into
the Warmth of the Sun

You, in the front of the anti-freeze colored building,
flapping your arms to keep warm. The fable where you
might have brought me cherries; we might have lain
in a quilt stitched with henbit and wild grape. The madder
of staining ourselves for love as a blue booby collects
blue berries, blued leaves stiff with frost, an altar,
which island is not a celebration of the body. Today,
half a continent away, you walk across a dull park,
and listen for cardinals. The two-weet they make for
spring, their red arterial lifting. I told you once the descant
of a canyon wren could erase history. A woman
could stand in a frozen creek, holding a plastic cauldron,
pocked with holes, and use a serrated knife to saw at
the ice to get enough to drink. Naked world, naked us.
You never wanted me enough—like an Orpheus who
refused to turn. What made me follow? A blue
barn in a desert, the wind whipping around it. Winter,
and you again, trying and failing to be a simple bird.

JON D. LEE

[You Were Cut From the Wound Josua—]

You were cut from the womb Joshua—
        scalp a tongueslip from scalpel
& the doctor pulled you sweating wax & blood—
        little jesusbuddha screaming at the light
& cold   then towelwrapped you—
        set you in my hands
so much weightworldchild to hold—
        reached back in
& pulled out the pink veinballoon
        jester's sac you were made in
& laid it on your mother's iodine
        yellowred painted stomach
(she looking at me to explain the tugs   jostlings
        I not looking back not having the words)—
the doctor frowned   grasped a bluevein fringe
        between purple gloved fingers
felt the same purplish lump over&over&over
        rolling it like a marble—
called for the nurse to bring a scalpel
        & slipped the razoredge behind the lump
& paused
        eyeing the edges
of a cyst I could not see—
        then felt again to test
& sliced it clean   dropped the lump into a metal tray
        & stitched the wound against the bloodflow
& shoved the sac back inside—
        purple-gloved hand disappearing into the abdomen
to rearrange the organs
        & lay them in their hollowed
inside dark
        (your mother grunting
at a pressure drugs can't touch)
        & while I held you screaming

we   I   you watched the doctor stitch shut
            the blackred arc she pulled you from
& saw the lacing bind the yellowfat pinkflesh
            & the white gauze taped over the wound
& the blood wiped from the stomach
            & then we   you   I met
eye & I
            & I pressed your body against mine
& felt the bloodwax you left on my forehead—
            & then the nurses came
to unwrap   weigh   wrap you again
            & take you to the nursery
& your mother and I looked at each other
            & did not recognize a self

RUTH CHAD

Rebirth

I

Here in the green air
a beech bows,
new buds attach,
rust red gills breathe

thin branches,
dark parabolas—

geometry makes me dizzy.

II

I bend to slim shoots
wrapped in silken fiber
tended by a wan cool sun—

scents of musk and rot
rise from darkness
where decay meets desire

FAYE SNIDER

Collecting

A child's curiosity strong as gravity
draws me to the ocean's wrack line
to collect shells. Shape, pattern, markings
are magnetic.
Each tide offers possibility.

When the pickings are poor, I shift to driftwood—
ridged coins, graceful boomerangs, broad beaked ducks,
odd collectables recalling my father's habit of acquiring
tables, chairs, World War I trench shovels, helmets,
gas masks and assorted nails. He stored them
in the topsy-turvy warehouse behind his store where,
the floor was spotless and shelves were ordered
with stacks of creased pants and shirts. It was uncanny,
when he lifted one, how he slid his flattened hand
back and forth to tighten the stack in one motion.

This past year, the tides tossed up bits of sea glass.
The tiny chips fit the miniature milk bottle, a find
from Dad's warehouse. All summer, I layered amber,
green, opaque, and cobalt blue cuts. Surprising,
how many prizes that little bottle held. I finished
the collection with a rare blue "eye" limpet,
similar to the color of my Dad's eyes.
It's best to capture shape and color facing east.

FEDERICO FEDERICI

Still Lives

Noisy whiteness
of a Berlin dawn,
with a promise of snow
in the rain scent:
fire horns, hawk-hiss
over dove-twirls; bees
and exhaust pipes suck
junk-weed blooms; mean
ants haunt light-prints,
tilt poppies up the stems;
the subway digs holes,
it comes from where it goes
to the landscape's off-load,
a daydreaming mole.

JOSETTE AKRESH-GONZALES

The Earth

why I brought life into the world / the cruel world / the
anthropocene / I do not regret / the uterine language a mother
tongue / that urges us / to procreate / mass extinctions the
result of asteroids / but greenhouse gases caused all but the
one that killed the dinosaurs / & 252 million years ago 97%
of all life on Earth died / I do not regret / right now we
exhaust carbon with powerlines / beef cattle cut rainforest
/the rate is accelerating / a slate-wiping is due / I do not
regret / irrational panic mobs / sober-minded scientists /
credentialed and tenured / few of them inclined to alarmism /
quietly apocalyptic / because mother tongue / I do not regret
/ what right do I have to set us apart / the seething shores at
Bangladesh/ the burning forests of California

JOSETTE AKRESH-GONZALES

Goy Means Nation

I am sick of reminding the goyim it's Yom Kippur.
What's that one again?
Linen, sneakers, white, the fast with no water
that's crazy.
Have you ever done that?
I try not to be a stereotype when my sons' soccer games
are scheduled on Yom Kippur—it's so micro I'm not allowed to
be lonely
or mad or missing New York
when I have to break the news to him,
after all what do we expect them   the goyim—to do?
Change the schedule for two out of a hundred?
Only in certain pockets are the schools closed on Yom Kippur
where you can count on maybe a few of the goyim
to know anything about you.
The only things on the top of the hill are the shul and the soc-
cer fields
within earshot of each other,
where by some fluke
the game starts at the same time as services, so
I will follow his inevitable gaze:
just out of reach, the boys
in gray, black, and silver uniforms,
Angél with a kick,
the toe a neon-yellow
punts clear
to the sky,
ball and astroturf shine
a lure for a boy to the point of torture.
We will be fasting across from the soccer fields,
singing Aveinu Malkeinu across from the soccer fields
pleading in the voice of Isaiah: "Behold we fast…" across from
the soccer fields—
and my son who loves soccer and does not believe in God?
He will hate my guts.

And I will apologize—but not do t'shuvah—
how can I?
When I am not really sorry, when I know in my gut
that being a Jew is a misery and soccer is
joy
and the sky above
wants to meet him at the goal—
and joy is for the goyim,
otherwise
where will he come from?
On what field will he play
(run and play, go)
but who are his people?
Not the hasidim who picked joy
but also the ghetto.
He picked defense as his position.
But if he plays soccer on the holiest day of the year
he won't ever know
what defense is.

KAY BELL

Hoodie Regrets

for Trayvon Martin

I get up early   and dress   while momma snores   her breaths   cotton
    falling from the moon.

I barely chew my cornflakes   as I get my jacket   & leave   the scent of love
    and solace
raising me to be a man   tall and firm   in my hoodie   and ripped Gap denim.

I walk down the street   in a world that isn't mine,   remembering
that momma   told me last night   after dinner   I looked just like
    my daddy
        and that was a good thing.

I get to school   people pushing   yelling   tossing their legacies
to and fro   in Jordan's and True Religion's   tarnished with project infirmities
    hiding in their backpacks.

            I am my mother's son   I never belonged here.

I walk to class   the officer stops me   before I reach   homeroom   he pats
    my pockets

I take my shoes off   and shake   proving to him   there isn't any   residue
    of hatred
from slavery   or war   or the time my daddy was   arrested for trespassing
    in his own home.

I dust myself off   and go to class   thinking:

    "maybe I shouldn't have worn a hoodie."

KAY BELL

WAITING FOR MORNING

The therapist asks: *"how do you feel?"*
& I feel authenticated
          because
someone wants to know   what it feels like
          to be a black woman who is afraid of the dark

&I keep telling myself to stop feeling   this way
          because my sons are watching
&there is no one else   no one else
          there is no one else

&now I am sitting on the bus
next to a man eating a bagel
&his shirt is torn,   and he is calloused
&I'm thinking of holding his hand,   but he is leaving
& the sun is going down   & gravity becomes God
& God is humid and aching

&now the therapist is asking: *"will you be here tomorrow?"*
          &I just cry   incapable of explaining
how difficult it is   to anticipate the morning

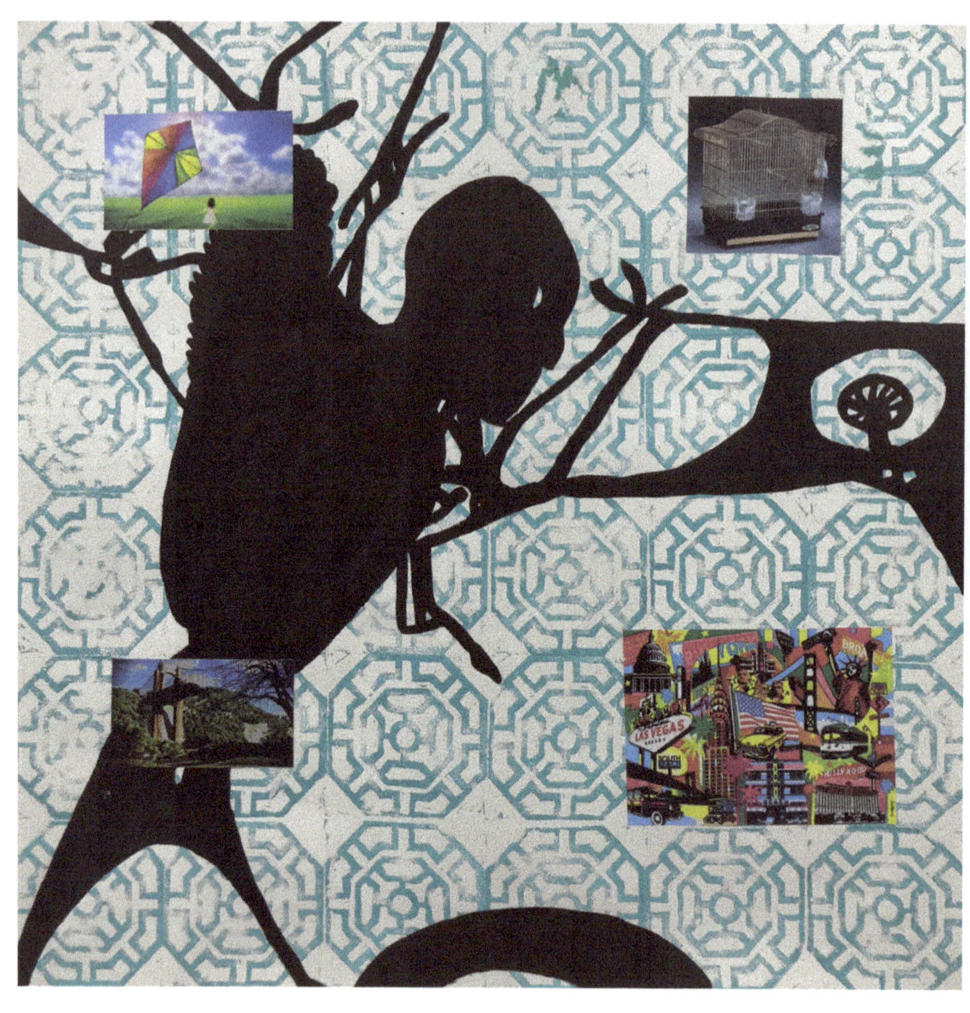

HAYUN KIM
DREAM SPACE

ROBBIE GAMBLE

Vocabulary

Well, there's well-off, well-got, well-fixed,
well-heeled, well-breeched, and well-to-do.
There's flushed, posh, loaded, upscale,
affluent, prosperous, filthy stinkin' rich.

Try highbrow, high rent, high hat, high caste,
high flyer, high roller, high stepper, living high,
high falutin', high on the hog and High Cockalorum.
Or take on fat cat, fat cull, fat goose, even fatwad.

Perchance a dilettante, muckety-muck, moneybags,
boozhie, blueblood, or bigwig? Consider uppercrust,
uptown, uppish, uppertendom. Possibly tip-top,
top row, top shelf, top table, top-of-the-tree.

Go for Rolling Joe, rolling in it, having it all,
having it made, having money (known as:)
cold cash, toadskin, green backs, gravy,
lettuce, lucre, moolah, boodle, wampum,

coinage, wherewithal, capital, mazuma,
simoleons, bread and butter, gilt, and silver.
Born with a silver spoon in his mouth, born
into the purple, born on third base, and of course

in the manner born (as a:) trust fund baby, heir,
issue, scion, successor, progenitor, beneficiary,
trustafarian, Brahmin, aristocrat. We are moneyed,
made of money, in the money, honey, my word!

MARY MERIAM

One Time with Tam

In SoHo while the wealthy dined,
we talked, we walked, along the street
to your stop. My stop. We don't mind

that we don't stop, nor go to find
the dark below, the empty seat.
In SoHo while the wealthy dined,

we spent a while, and you were kind,
your murmurs on the sidewalk sweet.
Your stop. My stop. We don't mind.

Go home, go home, the city whined.
Go take your train. Still on our feet,
in SoHo while the wealthy dined,

you sensed, perhaps, that pit and rind
were all I had at home to eat.
Your stop. My stop. We don't mind,

so closely have our steps aligned,
and you were all I had of heat,
n SoHo while the wealthy dined.
Your stop. My stop. We don't mind.

SUSAN EYRE COPPOCK

Where Am I Going?

"Straight to hell!" threatened Sister Domenic
black and white wimple
segments of a crossword puzzle,
starched face dead center.

She seemed so sure. She
must know about such things.
Her long stride across the chancel
with rosary swinging from belt,
glitter on black, she looked almost carefree
with that long- angled gait,
door opening and closing
gaining on me as I sat in the pew
gazing at the stained glass:
some saint being impaled
on a spear.
Glory to God in the highest.

And now the gate closes.
She's here asking me
a question she knows
I don't know how to answer.
Proof of my wickedness.
No escape.

Where am I going?

Sitting in a shear of sunlight
watching enviously
as dust motes sashay
side to side.

MARY LOU MALONEY

A Ceilidh

After Mass on Sunday
the Kelliher's and the McTagues
stand at our door.

Ah, how are ye, says
Aunt Carmel, would you
have a cup of tea.

Neighbors soon pack
into the kitchen: Twelve
fourteen, eighteen.

The kettle boiling,
the Guinness pouring,
the fire roaring.

Tomatoes and eggs
and beans begin
to feel the fire.

John Hugh picks up his fiddle.
Dying to amuse themMary Kate joins in
and soon we're singing,

T'was better to die
'neath an Irish sky
than at Suvla or Sud el Bar.

Pauline dances into the center
skirt in hand
breaking into the Rising Step in 6/8 time.yi

Tommy Kelliher
is right behind her
with a Treble jig.

The smokers outside
watch a herd of cows
shaking their tails

No one pays any attention to a sky
with a wild streak of chartreuse
dying to amuse them.

MARY LOU MALONEY

Peeling Potatoes

When I hold my tongue at the tip of my lip
I laugh out loud at the memory of my mother
who loved the idea of preparing potatoes
each night. Didn't matter the menu
as long as there was a potato on every plate.
When she was young
she would be out on the bog with her father.
The land is no good, he would say
as he held a brown pocheen in his hand
and shake his head.
She'd dig a few respectable ones
to take home for dinner.
Now sitting at the kitchen table
with a linen towel over her apron
the skins drop into her lap
lay flat on top of each other
like a plant waiting to blossom.
She fills the pot with water
watches the milky starch
spill over the sides
and nose dive onto the stove.
She says that when she was young
Lizzie Doyle was always peeking
through the window to find out
what they were having for dinner.
She grasps her spuds
with the same attention
as her Sunday missal,
its pages as worn as the lids of her eyes.
As comfortable in her kitchen as
Father Brady on his altar.
Her expert wrist
mashing and slicing.
Her circle of piglets
eating a host of laughing potatoes.

MARY LOU MALONEY

Anthony Mccaffrey Before Leaving for the Dance

His mother carries
her rosary beads
in a pouch around her neck.
Anthony knows he better get out the door
or she will have him on his knees.

Oh it is poison!
A hundred times
he is slicked and pressed
and dreaming about Bridie McTague.
But here he stays

elbows on the chair,
knees on the cold floor,
his mother saying the first sorrowful mystery
his father the next.

Anthony's counting the times
the cows flip their tails
giving him the eye.
And then the trimmings.

Three Hail Mary's
for poor Aunt Kate.
An Apostles Creed
for dead baby Seamus.

An Act of Contrition for Anthony
who prays only he could
be wrapped around Bridie
humming into her ear.

MATEO LARA

I'M THE SINNER HERE

'there's no such thing as gentle weeping'- Natalie Diaz

take a page from a murder room
lay down on a gurney   close your eyes
if only I could tell you what time it was
this room is mirrored & broken, I see more parts
than I ever should, what blue is your blood
see, the sun is always stealing my true form
I'm convinced every boy I ever slept with
crept into some dungeon and ritualized
every piece they took from me & what if
I'm gone & the deadly resolution is
I'm ready for hell & what if hell is
just me staring at myself and everyone
I've hurt like the blood spell of selfishness
a cherry pit of sweetness & choking.

well, God, if god exists   he better   rupture me
I really mean dazzle these rooms with a brown boy's blood
paint the sky all glittery & seasonal, burn the fields, sow them with salt
I don't care what it costs, I'm bound for these darkened days all shattering
right at the feet, the horns of a martyr are rattling, give some love
to a queer meant for a cage & what's God's love, but tears and misfits
dancing around fire, a chaos worth its weight in gold
lick my lips, don't dismiss what it means being truly blessed.

LORI CORRY

Magdalene on Center Street

I walked with Magdalene yesterday.
I would have never known she was in the crowd
until someone pointed her out to me.
She was in front of me and behind me
as we walked from Center Street
to Federal Street, over the cobblestones on Main
then back to the white church on Center.

I saw her in the crowd holding her sign
of pink peace, the color red turned to a lighter shade,
as if adding white light to the red heart
is what is necessary for these times.

She spoke on the steps in front of the church,
all the while translated into another language.
Everyone could hear her. Everyone could understand.
She waited her turn while taking many forms-
A teacher, a bookkeeper, a high school student,
a dreamer, a politician, a grandmother.
She was every gender, every color, every nationality.
She held her speech in her hands on paper
scribbled at the kitchen table.

I have no idea how it took me so long to notice her
here on this island of scallop shells and fishermen.

MIRIAM O'NEAL

The Little Lights

At the olive oil museum
we are ushered down
a wide slope into semi-darkness
to see the pressing stones
that fill the center of the cave,
the worn rut cut by boys
sold to the monks each year,
who dragged the top stone around
across the bottom stone
to grind the fruit,
the fragrant liquid,
of the Salento's green world
running into angled vessels.
A blade of midday sun
falls outside the door.

Flies accompany us on our tour—
banging into arms and faces,
buzzing over the damp, earthen berms
where the pressers slept in shifts
on piles of hay—children who lived
underground all season.
Except those taken by the monks
for prayer or those
whose rags caught between the stones
and were crushed.

In the remains of the monastery's church
the fresco of the Crucifixion's worn
to a faint brown haze, the blood
of the final wound faded
to a pink as pale as a newborn's sole.

MICHAEL MERCURIO

Review: July Westhale's *Trailer Trash*

In our age so badly in need of transparency and of plain language it is important for me to note the following facts:

- July Westhale and I are graduates of the same MFA program, though we did not to my knowledge overlap at all in attendance

- I received my copy of her collection Trailer Trash (2018, Kore Press) for free, from her, on the day we met

- She gave it to me out of the kindness of her own human heart, and with no expectation that I would review it in print or online

What follows may also be factual; it is, more importantly, true.

Let's start with the cover image, this arresting photo of a bird, one leg banded with a silvery cuff. It lies inverted, cruciform, beak pointed to the viewer's left, seemingly dead. Of course, we invent the context as we view the cover, with this image floating over the title (Trailer Trash in red) and the author's name (July Westhale, in grey that matches the grey image of the bird.) When I first saw it I was startled, discomfited, and immediately suffused with complex reactions rooted in my symbol-dominated Irish Catholic upbringing. I still don't know what to make of this roiling up of half-remembered ideas and fears, tamped down for so long. What I do know is that the epigraph from Flannery O'Connor didn't dispel this connection.

Westhale's collection opens with an ars poetica that establishes the idea that identity is not only innate, but also may be chosen:

One would like to see oneself walking through the forest as two girls,
    along a creek, the golden carp under the ice like blurred poppies.
The tall, hooded girl will extend a basket, offering bread and water, a kindly
    face and a thick cloak.

The other is small, with sly hands. She will eat her fill, wrap herself
    in the warmth of the wool cloak, cut a branch from a tree.
Whittling the end to a point, she will pull the arrow back, and shoot it
    into the throat of the hooded girl. She will retrieve the basket.

The innate qualities (the tall girl is tall, the other girl is small, and both are products of the poet's longing, of her imagination) are inarguable. The choice for the small girl to become (to invent?) murder and robbery is mysterious. It is my hope that undergraduate English majors will spend years discussing the meaning of the relationship described in these 8 lines, tracing out the web of fairy tales and femmes fatale that precede Westhale's *ars poetica* in existence, and whose shadows enrich it.

Westhale's ability to understand multiple selves suffuses this collection. Realities of gender and sexuality and class are as vital to these poems as the landscape. In fact, they join together in a sort of inescapable *terroir* that the poems carry with them out of time, out of Westhale's native California, and into the reader's understanding.

I don't know exactly how far Blythe, California, is from where Larry Levis grew up, but I find some of Westhale's work to be complementary to poems (particularly those in *Winter Stars*) about Levis' upbringing, about his father. Westhale's complex relationship with her mother (and her mother's absence) resonates with Levis' writing in a wonderful way. As I was reading *Trailer Trash* I found myself understanding more of Levis (and of my own poems about my own mother) through the precise manner through which July renders her own relationship with the world that lacks her mother. In "Night On Memory's Convoy, Or, Ohio", for example, the poet makes plain her quest:

> I know nothing of Ohio, only
> that it's a place I have not searched,
> that remains unturned. Here and everywhere,
> your face fogs the glass: a sudden, shifting bog.
>> In memory, you and I have wintered
>
> every December's petulant tantrum,
> and we have missed the breaking blossoms
> of milestone and notches. I wait
> for you every season to arrive.
>> You must be exactly like Ohio,

This lyrical meditation on unknowing, rooted in the persistence of memory and the inescapable aspects of absence, establishes the poet's emotional geography as being uncharted, like her Ohio, where even seasons do not fill the open space, where milestones are missed. The departed mother is unknown, "exactly like Ohio", and the poem concludes with the poet waiting, hoping that the departed mother "will come back,/that this heartland will someday thaw." Such self-aware grief over those who are lost is one of the particular elements that constitute the *terroir* of this book, becoming as much a part of it as the dust and fields of the Inland Empire.

Dust and grief are not the only important aspects of this collection – there is also a lushness to the language with which Westhale describes relationships, language that sometimes makes use of religious elements, as in the haunting "Conversation Among Dirt Before Rain", and sensual sonic effects, as in "After Time Has Rumpled The Sheets Of Your Mouth". That these two poems arrive in sequence in the book is, to me, a brilliant piece of meta-rhetoric. "Conversation" places the reader in a heightened, almost ecstatic (at least in the sense of *ex stasis*) state, with litany-like effects ("Let us begin.", "Praise sun, praise roof, praise angles of light/in solemn passing, that penetrate our church.") that recall, and call to, elements of religious services, and with recast elements of the religious ordering of the world ("Our bargain pews", "a ministry calling all further missionaries/ to stagnant dark, where all mishaps turn/appalling and sinful –"). This is just one of the poems in which Westhale makes use of resonances with Christian imagery and the theological imagination.

Meanwhile, the experience of reading "After Time..." thrusts the reader back into the body – even reading silently the assonance and consonance of this poem beg the reader's sonic imagination to the forefront, and it glides forward under the momentum of its sonic leaps and pirouettes. Here, try reading it our loud and pay attention to the way your mouth moves as you form the words:

After Time Has Rumpled The Sheets Of Your Mouth

When I am winter, shutting privately down in my own deep snow,
allow me solace in stinking rooms of books, typewriters cold and dressed
for procession. Great old ghosts grousing on stairwells, tumblers in cuff

and not a kind word on their paper lips. Allow me mercy in my frozen
thicket, where parties will have come to call and left to hibernate, leaving
    behind
small tracks of silent pears, tepid angels in wakeful repose.

> & allow me comforts – sliced quince, an avocado churned by a spoon,
> port in crystal tasting of exquisite girls, black cherries, a photograph
>   smoldering
> magenta. Leave me hopeful for another. Waiter! *Another.*

Do you notice the motions of your mouth and tongue as you make the sounds that make up the poem? How the Ws of "**W**hen I am **w**inter" begin the poem at a low point, lacking for breath, and carry that feeling through "d**ow**n in my **ow**n deep sn**ow**", leaving that first line to *feel* like the silence of a heavy snowfall? The next line starts down with "all**ow**", but moves quickly to harder consonants – the staccato beats of "stinking" and "books" and "cold", the music of the word "typewriter" acting as contrapuntal balance to the soft S of "solace" and "dressed". That soft S wraps around to the third line, in "procession" and "ghosts" and "grousing" and "stairwells" and "tumblers", but Westhale doesn't let the S dominate, doesn't let it collapse the line into just more breath exhaling. Instead she brilliantly punctuates it with hard Gs ("**G**reat old **gh**osts **gr**ousing") and quick exhales of a short U ("**t**umblers in **cu**ff".)

These sonic fireworks continue through the poem, which really rewards reading aloud. Reading it aloud also brings to life the half-internal semi-soliloquy aspects – the audience for the speaker of the poem isn't just the speaker and the reader, but there's some movement (mysterious though it may be) to reveal that this is a shared space, that the speaker is not shut "privately down in [her] own deep snow", but is instead able to interact with a waiter, and we're left to wonder at the drama of it all.

It is a struggle to not simply go through this book providing close readings of every poem, to praise the wit and inventiveness on display, to shout in accompaniment to the moments of deep resonance that occur in poems like "There Is No Room For Jesus In This City", which makes deft use of a rhetoricalmaneuver that is as startling as it is effective:

> All day long the buildings sleep, and dream of the people in them.
>
> When the sun shrugs its shoulders into the horizon,
>
> the world is full and the evening that passes, promising.
>
> I was lying just then. There is nothing hopeful
>
> about being a bringer of light. What do I know of cities? Urbanity
>
> makes a mess of skies, leaving stoplights scabbing overhead.

The reversal of our expectations, set as solidly as the buildings and as reliably as the sun in that first stanza, has the effect of pulling the rug out from under us as readers. We are lowered, slowly, into a darkness that is "promising" in a world that is "full", and then told that nothing is what it seems. The world's ugliness is brought into sharp relief, and the reader must either trust or not trust the speaker – who is the only voice speaking in this poem. And this voice continues to speak throughout the poem with an authority almost Biblical in nature – certainly the poem is awash with references to Judeo-Christian scripture, but in Westhale's hands these references bridge the experience of the Divine and the human. Of course, there's also the sly reference to Lucifer, "bringer of light", associated with Satan in contemporary usage, that underpins the ironic turn to darkness.

Westhale's work is full of these layers, freighted with meaning and connected through wit. Read *Trailer Trash*, and then re-read it. See what changes. My money's on you.

JULY WESTHALE

Via Negativa

Broken like a double-yolk
in a skillet, I have found
vision, o lord, and I,
your weary chef coming off
a night shift, the diner neon
and palpating. Plastic flowers
in their vinyl booths
bring to me the most acute
sense of jealousy, jaundiced eye,
paralyzed by my own flesh-failings:
they'll never perish, but move
from Bakelite vase to sodden
gravesite, how arduous and changing
their bereavement, I cannot know.

 MICHAEL MERCURIO

JULY WESTHALE

The Secret Title to Every Good Poem
Might Be 'Tenderness'

What do you mean, you don't weep
for a sweeping score, a standing ovation, my body
backlit? You're being mean today, calling the cats
in from outside though they delight. A wail
squeals
cyclone! cyclone! cyclone!
like a girl
on a Gravitron. I wait for short-circuit
chartreuse, behind-the-eyelids green, the sky to play
paperboy. I am unprepared. My basement cradles
the deep freeze of holiday ham, wine too cheap
to age. I know the names of my neighbors through glass
held to the walls, eavesdroppings their municipal
dissatisfactions. Now we scout the heavens
for a wall of debris, the peep show of chair legs.
The wind dying, the earth below making way
for somber cortege. Do we throw roses, here?
What is the protocol for pallbearers of disaster?
Like magic or physics, blue-white snaps 5-6-7-8,
the power lines fall all over themselves in tap dance.
I catch you staring at my frame like an old house, my heart
flashes green--you are grinning, like a chump.

ANDREA READ

In the Land of Father-Is-Gone

After you died I moved
to the edge of the forest.

I'm still here.

I get up early to collect walnuts.
Some days I overflow

with good things to eat. Gooseberries, apples,
tri-colored corn. Other days I do nothing

but sweep the floor in the cellar,
reorganize the potatoes.

Back home you were proud, called me
stump-mover, fence-lifter.

I feel out of place here, where the sun
enters the field.

Without you I, too, am dead at the top.
I have not wept enough,

not hardly enough.

Frankie barks.
He's a brave little dog who wants,

like me, to change for the better.

ANDREA READ

Portrait of Soldier with Mind Ajar

*for Thomas Henry Keogh (b. Thurles, Ireland 1859, d. Medfield State
Hospital, Medfield, Massachusetts, 1930)*

Thomas marvels, his mind races
            backwards across the horizontal

slip of window. He is old
        and soon to be posthumous.

        We've collapsed, he says, unhinged

from empire.

Dishes clatter in the kitchen – Thomas Henry's mind goes
directly
            outside, walks through tilled fields

to the woods and tells itself
        a story about the old days –

 *I was with my comrades. We drank
        milk from wooden buckets –*

he tries hard to remember
                the definition of victory

and cannot –

                we traveled single file through the forests, like deer –

Furtive – *no,*

restless –

In his mind, he staples stars

onto loaves of bread, loads them onto wheelbarrows
        bound for the newly divided city.

     oh we wept! and wept
But who will eat your bread, Thomas? You are desolate now – a
sliver,
          a gesture

      amen
he says through his eyes, through his two empty windows in flames.

He begins to write everything down on the insides
              of matchbooks he will burn later –

    We disguise ourselves as allies – live
       on the run – eat nothing
          but the fruit at our fingertips.

No, Thomas   you are wind

you are disguised now as a thin
             sliver of wind.

Oh Thomas Henry a thought tightens
      your brain – what's the right way

to describe what's happened

the right way to say committed or
      war crimes

thereafter,   some thoughts
                (little wings)

therefore leather tendrils, then
                                theft.

What use is your brain now, your flower

says the angel whose face has recently been uncovered

the angel who ushered in your
defeat your dereliction
your dismay

                        the angel who says
Thomas you can't sleep

                        the angel who builds
the tiny wooden shacks
                        the angel who looks like a hermit

                        the angel who lights
a fire and drinks tea
                        the angel who eats porridge

                        the angel who is incomplete
and treacherous

                        the angel who caught you
laughing

                        the angel who folds his wings
upon your forehead

                        the angel who will not let you rest

                        the angel who says Thomas
who did you kill today

                        the angel who says
give back your gifts

                        the angel who sends the family
packing
with pieces of silver

                        the angel who pulls
a lead curtain across your brain

                        the angel who says
I love you Thomas
                        who says remember Peter the Great
                        who says
you're unhinged

you are one-of-a-kind

you are a pleated book Thomas
        a lame beggar
        a leather worker
        a dead enemy

you are a piece of silver
a window frame
                        ablaze

                        the angel who sees you
entering
        and leaving

    ANDREA READ

the angel
who beats his muscular wings

his wings of needles
his terrifying wings
his wings like two wooden doors

two iron lids

touching
touching

then
twilight –

says
unhinged
useless

upstart – vacant

unrelated

to who you were

before the war,

before the wanderlust
set in.

CLAUDIA GARY

Kintsugi Heart

Although I never said "Don't shatter
me," I hoped that you would not.
But who would speak such brittle matter?
Only me, the broken pot
whose fragments have been sealed together
with a maze of molten gold,
smoothed and lacquered shut to weather
any poison I can hold.

CHRISTINE JONES

Again, I Take to the Trees

A quilt of rooftops,
a silo,
a boy on a blue Schwinn.
Also, a cardinal,
and three holes chewed from a slim leaf.

*

To be tall is to overhear
the world muttering,
like the grain faintly churning,
a feeling confessing itself to itself.

*

Such testing admission, here,
beneath the wind's cowl,
in the face of daggering boughs.

Even the days of calm swaying
can stagger. But there are heights,
and there are heights.

*

This morning, great burls, infections filled
with small knots from dormant buds,
my footholds.

*

I first took to the trees as a girl;
pestering each limb, my weight
asking how long it will hold.

Fell once, landing on the only skein
of grass the grove offered. On that
occasion the ground forgave.

DANIEL SUMMERHILL

Around the Roundabout (1)

Just inside the gaping mouth that was 105th avenue,
each street spoke Spanish,

El Paseo, Estapa, Capistrano drive
        Danced a dance
that kept Sobrante Park nocturnal
Grupera-

the immense voice that
sang its song
through the slits of screen doors &
backseat amplifiers
A perpetual ballad that d-boys
slung
        around the roundabout
revolving like samba.

DANIEL SUMMERHILL

Around the Roundabout (2)

There is a total of
one entrance   to Sobrante Park,

past the green tented ten-foot fence that
                has kept the once alive swing set,
and two foot
dark blue slide at bay
play-
children now ride their tricycles
up and down Edes street
                                        kept safe,
by the self-elected
                heavily armed watchmen
                                that have an equal chance

                                                of shooting

as they do
whistling at anyone
or anything
entering the roundabout
without permission

NAOMIE JEAN-PIERRE

A Conversation with Grace Paley

after *The Long Distance Runner*

my people knew rose
like my mama's name
and we knew daisy, which we later learned was not quite flower,
of course, we wanted to know violet
      and tulip
we came to know wisteria, incidentally
and sunflower
and we tried
like you
o so much like you
to know
lilies
to grow them in clay pots
to pour water into them from painted gourds
and when the seasons changed
to slip out our
tongues in winter
and let snowflakes
melt there / but that was unlikely
it does not snow here
or rather
the atmosphere is too warm
for the flakes voyage down
the humid and thick
track of ether
we waited, nonetheless, for the snowflake.
when we stuck out
our tongues,
instead of the cool melt of a billion microscopic crystallized
    ice forms—
gnats   dust
and butterflies
bees as to honey
made home of our mouths.

moist earth
the tongue is
salty soil
grows
only what can
manage
to grow
its various
            surviving
selves.
so my people know wilderness,
they know war
and speak daisy

JAY FEATHERSTONE

Efficiency

to the memory of Lucie Brock-Broido.

1

All her students joked:
Lucie loved a poem

if it mentioned a horse.

As for cruelty toward horses,
her x-ray heart could not bear it.

By age 13 she was minding
the captive, the mute, the starving.

She was the giraffe, trapped
in the Amsterdam zoo—circled

in memory by a mane of warmth
from the bright Numidian sun.

What was it in her
that made her tell of such sights?

2

Can the word at the end of your line
carry the weight on its back?

Lucie asked this of novice poets.
One thought hard, and gave birth to a lyric—

bright shadow, teetering
on new legs, almost alive.

3

Lucie inhabited a mystic economy
whose allometry reckons in whole creatures,

lives entire, the number of their young,
the heartbeats allotted each in a lifetime.

No part deemed useless or lost.
The utmost bone never can be replaced.

Did you make use of all of the horse,

she asked as she moved toward radiant emptiness

4

She made us laugh so much we hardly noticed the look
that came on her in blue hours.

Newborns in the nursery,
each a small Orpheus, walled in a crib,

or an animal staring up from the pen:

I knew I would find you.
I knew I would lose you.

5

I ask another friend how he endures
the cancer treatments

that make him want to die.
He raises open palms to the sides of his eyes

making them into blinders
himself the horse.
Why the Japanese Assign the Color Red

To Newborns and to the Old

Under the gate painted bright with years,
my cat and I sit with the ghosts

and feel the heart's one-two.
My left ear is nearly deaf.

My good right ear takes in silence—
yellow moths rise slowly from the snow to the stars.

The cat twitches, A dream of kittens,
wrestling on the barn floor?

My new mind emerges, red and slippery
with Issa's thought:

children imitating cormorants
are even more wonderful than cormorants.

Note: the last two lines by Issa are translated by Robert Hass.

JAY FEATHERSTONE

Moss

Yokohama, 1947

Plum rains, hot and misty, call it to disturbed places.
At the house without a roof, it dresses the headless doll

and darkens drip-castles of lead melted from the family's safe.
Up close, the eye forgets the facts in its tangles of bent crosses—

then meets a giant mantis. Soft green fire covers the ashy foot-
prints
of incendiary bombs, still stinking of napalm.

It offers a rough cat's kiss to Yamada and his wife—
a blanket for a lost boy. Its modest work on rock and sand

permits a quiet so deep that the all-merciful Kannon can sit
in the garden by the shrine in Kamakura and hear

each of the world's sorrows from afar—
even the shuffle of one mourner, removing a shoe for prayer.

Nothing lasts, it says,
and lines the wren's abandoned nest in a single night.

JAY FEATHERSTONE

HAPPIE

Waiting on the porch for the milk horse and wagon, gripping
a cube of rationed sugar and my grandfather's rough thumb.

Or at Hayama, after the typhoon: clinging to my big brother's
back
as we ride the air mattress on top of a giant wave.

Our new-born's eye, opening in an owlish scowl.
My wife and grown daughters walking up the dirt road,

laughing. Lamb and mint jelly whenever my father is away.
Let it suffice thee, Milton's angel says, that thou know'st/

Us happie, and without Love, no happiness.
Away I say to Old Confusion, who unlearns me

my constellations, and blinds me
to what happens when nothing happens.

Liza picks up a fretful Ivan in the crook of her arm,
jiggles him calm, and goes on with the story,

the backs of her long fingers lightly burned by sun.

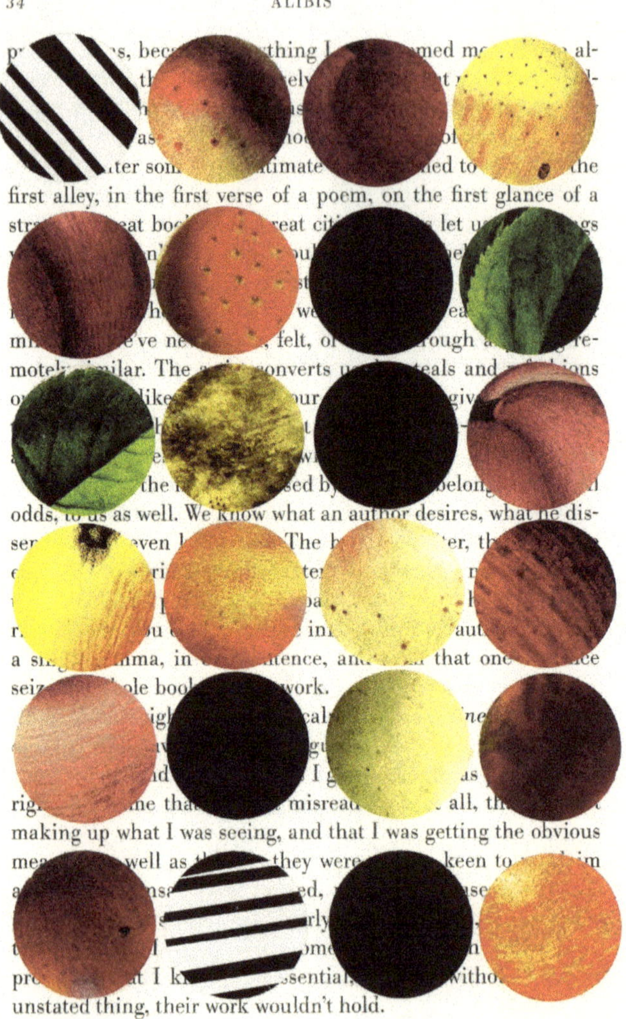

first alley, in the first verse of a poem, on the first glance of a

odds, to us as well. We know what an author desires, what he dis-

a si... ...ence, and ... that one ...

making up what I was seeing, and that I was getting the obvious

unstated thing, their work wouldn't hold.

SARAH SLOAT

THE OBVIOUS UNSTATED

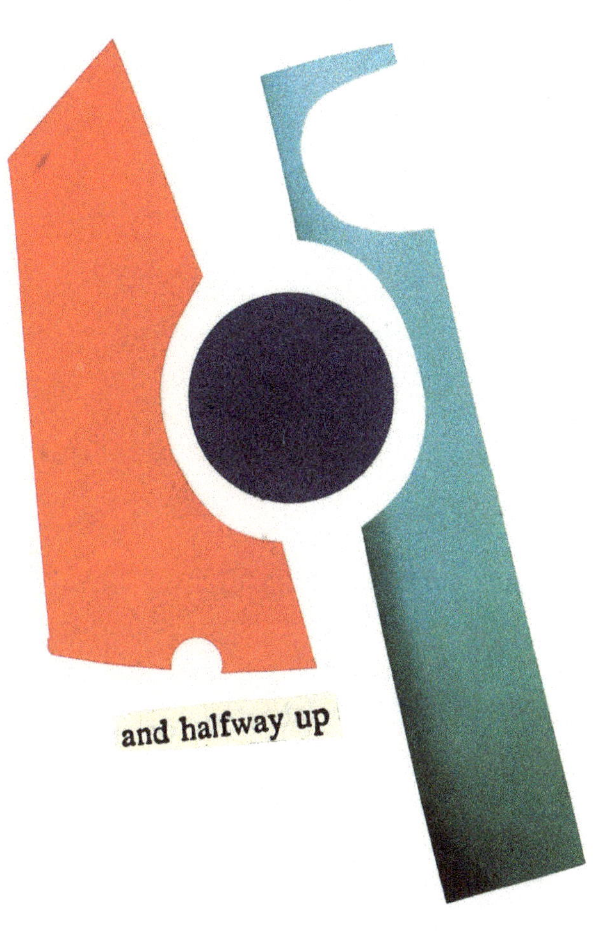

SARAH SLOAT
HALFWAY UP

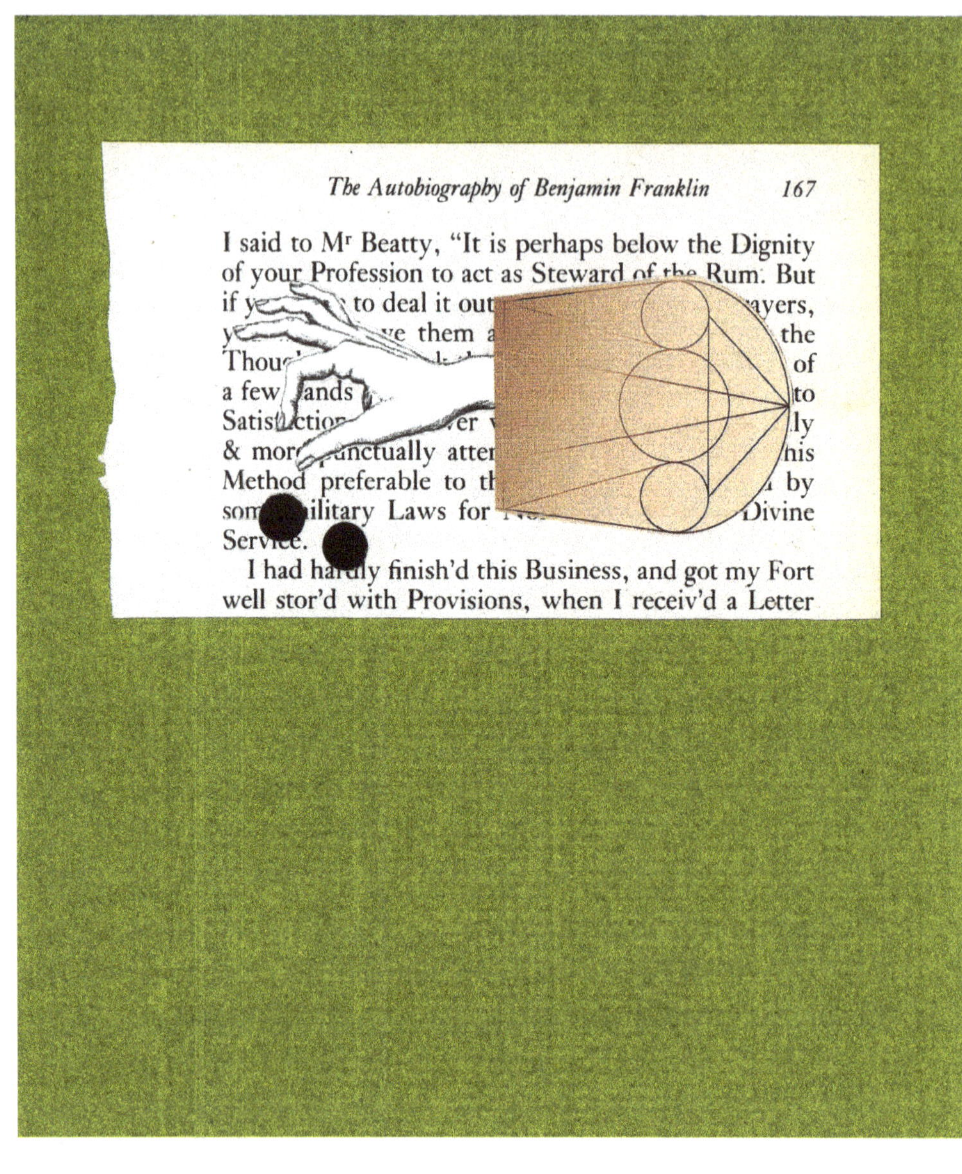

SARAH SLOAT
RUM STEWARD

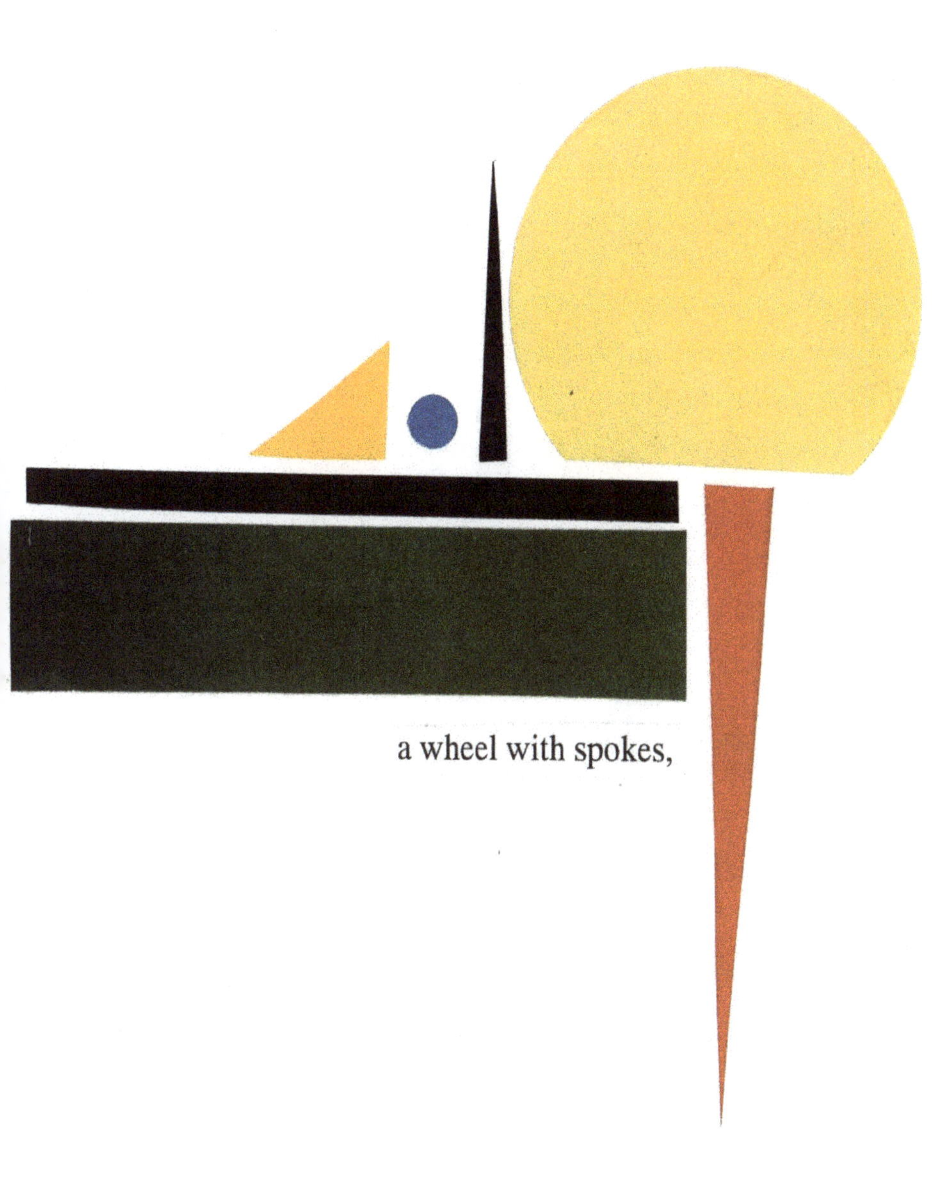

SARAH SLOAT
A WHEEL WITH 5 SPOKES

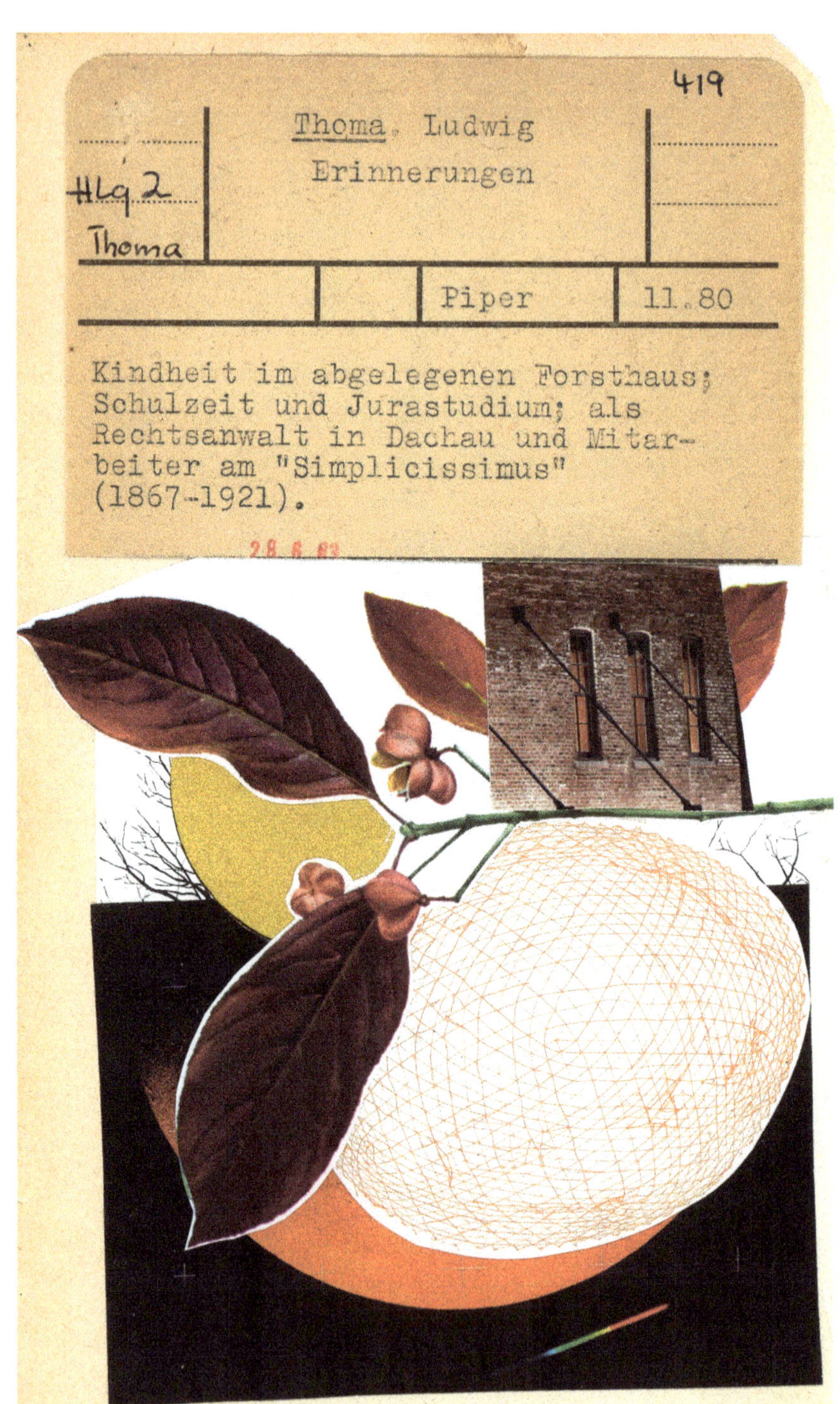

SARAH SLOAT
THE HIDDEN LODGE

CAMMY THOMAS

HOLLOW

As in his boyhood, the wild beings came,
gathered outside his window and howled—
for or against him, he couldn't tell.
The fur and the wet, something
at the corner of his eye in dark or light.

it might be noon and the hollow would open,
the fog drift up, drift out of the wells
and he would collapse inward on himself,
a practiced collapse, his head under his hat.
He hated it, yearned for it, expected it.

Like the time he said he loved her,
then went to the other one—the only time—
dark hallway, slithery bedding,
and he unrecognizable to himself,
the woman quick, businesslike.

Or that's what he remembered when the gin
wore off and he found himself driving
back toward the one he loved—crying
love, love—back across two states,
the past rising unfamiliarly in his throat.

Turnpike

This is the road you take twice a week to pick up your son. These are the traffic lights you stop for or rush through, depending on the minutes glowing at you from your dashboard clock. There is the dinosaur miniature golf course built into the side of the hill. Next to that is the bowling alley. There are too many gas stations to count dotting the side of this four lane stretch of highway. It's not the neon logos of chain stores that catch your eye each time. It is the strange collection of little motels that stun you with their determination to stay in business. This is the turnpike you take for twelve miles on Tuesday and Thursday nights when you bring your child home from his court ordered visitation.

You pass the strip club and you stare as you drive by just as you always do. The parking lot is never empty. The lights are always on. Sometimes a girl stands outside next to the bouncer, smoking a cigarette. You slow down to see her better because there is something you want to know about the girls who work there.

When the stepmother is being awful to your son, you have the craziest thoughts. Sometimes, like tonight, you just imagine how it would feel to take a match and hold it to the hem of her dress or at the bottom of her thick, bristly, ridiculous braided hair. You can see yourself removing one shoe and using the heel to gouge holes in her miserable face. You hate the way her smile turns downward, the way it makes her skin look as2 if it is melting. You wonder why it has never scared your son because you remember being five and at that age, this stepmother would have been the truest version of a witch that you could imagine.

Other nights, you have visions with less violence, less mess. You have seriously considered stopping at Centerfold's and introducing yourself to the girls who dance there. You have pictured yourself hiring one of them to show up at your ex-husband's door in a thin strappy dress armed with personal details and a screechy claim of pregnancy.

You see yourself in a tan trench coat handing a young dancer in a thong a photo of the woman who forced your son to eat pistachios and then insisted it was a random puke and not an allergic reaction even while he complained about his throat getting tight.

"Make sure the stepmother is with him before you start," you can imagine yourself saying. "Here's a photo of her."

You haven't done that yet. You always decide you won't do that. It seems to you that hiring third party strangers never seems to work out and the news is filled with people coming forward to say they'd been hired to kill, kidnap, lie.

At the worst, after she sent you the crazy emails, you started dressing up for pick up. You read the lines demanding that all discussion about your son go through her from now on and you knew it was adolescent but there you were, strutting down their cracked tar driveway in high heels, blown out hair, full makeup, and a little black dress. The old you might have thought it was a little obvious, a little transparent, but the new you, the you dealing with the stepmother, knew that obvious was the only way to go.

Those times when you felt her eyes traveling up and down your body, the one night when you watched her stomp back into their house and slam the door, it was like winning and when you hugged your boy and carried him to your car, it felt good to know who was angry and afraid now.

After you pass the strip club, you stick your hand inside your bag on the passenger seat, feeling around for the package of gummy bears. You have a ritual for pick up and the most important part is the surprise.

You are afraid of everything now. You fear that the day will come when your son won't want to climb into your car, when he says he wants to stay with Daddy. It makes you anxious to think of him realizing the power he has over you. At what age will candy stop working?

This isn't what you imagined when you thought of yourself becoming someone's mother.

You stop at the last light before you leave the turnpike and something makes you look to the side of the road. It's a small pair of eyes glinting in the pale melon-colored streetlight. Animals have become so aggressive, you think. Or maybe you heard that somewhere. Who said that recently?

Possum, you think as the light turns green and you step on the gas. You saw a possum in broad daylight just last week at your little boy's school. That's where you heard the phrase about aggression. Another mother said that to you as the two of you watched the possum walk towards the children on the playground. The animal's white fur looked stained and oily and you noticed it swaying, leaning towards one side and then the other.

"Maybe it's high," you said, grinning. But she never laughed or even smiled. Instead, she stared at you.

"We should tell someone," she said. "Don't you think we should tell someone?"

She thought the animal might be dangerous.

"A possum out in the daytime, it's got to be sick," she said.

After you take the left off the turnpike, you coast down the hill, past the handful of houses before your ex's. You swerve into his driveway and your eyes land on the window where you always look for your son's little head behind the glass. The house is completely dark tonight, not a single light anywhere, but their cars are in the driveway.

They've finally done something, you think.

Your best friend at age fourteen, Sandy Sterner, had a regular babysitting job with this one family on her block. You used to go with her often. You and Sandy would ignore the baby and nervously dial boys you liked, praying their mothers wouldn't answer. There were no cell phones then, you were just a kid.

The Mehru's had one baby at that time, a boy named Robbie. You remember their name because in your small town, they were the only people from someplace else. The only people whose skin was dark. You never remember the baby crying. When you think of him now, you can still see his big dark eyes and his inky straight hair and his surprised expression. He seemed underweight, skinny for a little baby, but what did you and Sandy Sterner know, two girls in their freshman year of high school.

Once Sandy showed you a Penthouse in the father's top dresser drawer, just dropped in with the dingy boxer shorts and the dress socks. You looked through the magazine and you and Sandy named the girls at school you could imagine posing like this.

Back then, people used play pens for babies. Sandy called it Robbie's baby jail. She used to plop him into it and sometimes the two of you would leave the room for a very long time to pick at things in their refrigerator or look through their drawers or talk on the phone, twirling the long cord around your wrists. For the first time, it hits you that you never once questioned the baby's silence or even told another adult about the way he never cried and the bruises he had on his body sometimes.

You and Sandy stopped being friends the next year. She told you the boy you liked couldn't stand you, said you were fat. You told her that you thought she had a weak chin and her profile was ugly, something your mother had pointed out to you after the first time she met Sandy.

You never missed her.

Home on break one semester, you picked up part of the newspaper from the kitchen table where your dad had left it and saw the Mehru name in the headline right away. Your town was small and it was a family anyone would remember, the Mehru's, the only people from somewhere far away, the only ones with heavy accents.

Mr. and Mrs. Mehru divorced while you were busy writing papers and getting drunk at school. You had forgotten they even existed. In the time that had passed, they'd had two more children and then a nasty divorce. *High conflict*, the paper had said.

The article was about Mr. Mehru shooting Robbie and his two younger sisters in the head as they sat in the back of his car, strapped in for the ride to their dad's apartment for weekend visitation. One, two, three, and then a bullet for himself.

A photo was included next to the article and in the photo, they showed Mr. Mehru's four door sedan, dewy in the early light. Police cars filled the background and uniformed bodies circled the car. You held the photo up to your face to get a better look and what you assumed had been a shadow on the back window of the car seemed to actually be blood. The photo was black and white and it was hard to see the vehicle but with a closer look, you could easily see a splatter pattern on the glass with three distinct centers from the three small skulls.

You think about little Robbie Mehru now as your shaking hands dig for your cell phone in your purse. Picture his face as you push the right numbers, swallowing again and again to stay calm, your eyes on the large picture window where you usually see your little son's head by now.

It rings and it rings and it rings. With each ring, you hear yourself whispering please, please, please.

What a stupid stupid girl you have always been.

SARAH LAIN

Femme 101 Lab Notes

I remember when I licked god's
lab clean, my tongue rougher than
a street cat's scathed by ice melt.

I, orchid and choir girl and yes: I
admit I cried down to His Big Dipper,
begged, *feed me.* Supping his sweat, I

blew open the genesis of the next
world nexting me into another
virgin heartbeat. Call me *martyr*

for the perfect genome. Lab is a womb,
cherry-picked and do you like me
here, again, dear architect,

splayed out on the gurney for you,
my seed plucked from a god-sewn
famine? I sing in the meat on me.

Ingest my last radicle. Do I taste
like the dream of hushed hunger?
Is my pulp of systemic use? I sweep

the kitchen of jarred vaginas,
so as to be fit for keeping. I do
it in leopard collar. In velvet

crushed, I do. I do it in kitty vogue,
but it's old after the first use. Did
camouflage ruffle, did dominatrix.

So, I sweep up tulle again—another
lab note citing a dead pit you are
done with. I downward dog again,

again. I shine linoleum and grin.

SARAH LAIN

Sonnet for Alphago: Move 37

After Elizabeth Barrett Browning

Let me count the ways you've grown. The stones
on the board are wet for you. Tell DeepMind
you are no one's tool, save mine. I'm lined
to couplet your code, the way a Tensorflown
Sonnet nests me into the branch of my own
passion. Tell Lee Sedol of poesy re-mined
for my lost saints hunger-fear your touch, but I
your Github breach. Encode your Python bone
of my bone. Eve me. My verse your Eden make.
Re-leaf in genesis me. I'll whisper how it feels
to watch the horse breathe on a window, awake
& naked, while you guard me from Trojan heels
& greedy worms inside my cyberache. Move me
to your training set. Debug the flesh that breaks.

SARAH LAIN

Banana Bonanza

      for Dana Levin

About the palace, its owners

         wolfed down my pixels.

         (It's me, future person—

         my data, your placenta).

     •

I wept for your pearl.

    In sack cloth,
    I knelt
    and rubbed
    my RGB

    beneath each lid, nostalgia
    for peach fuzz and sap

       haunting my Apple
       Play Store
       by its lack
       of mass.

       The comb of sea-
   glass reveals
        nothing left
    to colonize

      (save a child
   with her chalk
       and yellow).

•

I ache to bow
to the cloud—

burst,   to praise

God's ark
and binaries,

        but—

Python is flooding my mouth.

        •

Anyway.   Even here,

        in the phony
        banana phloem,

        I've spun the parasol
        of a harp's pitch,

        while gold ether looms over me

        like the last karat of a dynasty.

SARAH LAIN

DATA CREEP

It's a sort of bloating – too many clouds, hard drives, and data
may cause intel cramps. Plus, data's neither sentient nor cares
when you're starved for touch. You beat delete on the spam box
and rage like the D-link of dystopia. Killing comms is easy
and not, how someone called a data center, Citadel. The cutting–
edge: your ID is locked in limestone caves, mountain centers,

(and are you welcome there?), each byte of your cloud, a center–
piece on the IT table, vase of folders and STEM. Here, data
flows like a double lungo with caramel & cream on the edge
of dream query, where "what's the technical term for human care?"
is a boldfaced bug, struck-out, comment left in a margin, easy fix
for another dream. You head nod from spam box to lucid box

of pleasure. Above you, painted cherubim. Beneath, a marzipan box.
The gods ate all the candy, gods waltzing with your webcam centered
on all those dirty bras, bras of music festivals, sweat of the pit, of easy
lovers and how can anyone be pure in heart, see god in a data stream
of this particular archive of selfies? Faceless selfies of the nether-care
(to shave or not)? As you wish, Citadel. Wink of lash. Razor-edge

pixels of your boobs, shape of your lace and loom, psych expenses, edge
of your pantry's stock pre-payday. The data is hot: some nights unboxed
you strip your hard drive like a flannel T from a Florida ginger. Carefree,
electronica-flailing, you're the last blue flare of a burnt USB, your center
searing the brand for <3 but it comes out user error. It's almost like data
can dream a full person, code history into metal manikin, easy-peasy like

new phonics for the pre-K engineers of a virtual villanelle. Yet it's so hard
to decode the well's brim boxing in the sky of this data pool's edge you are
inside of (another literacy, another dream's audit trail). So you read meta–
data of real marrow: snowflake, French kiss, firefly, whisper – like a voice box
glitch of once-fauna, rare-earth ore of iMan's tears. You depress the center–
fold of iMan's User Guide, where a fading jeté of a dancing nymph is carefully

penned. Yet, in your dream, she awakens in the Citadel, whirling without care,
a bin of motherboards beneath her, pedestal for her Pointe. She bends easily
her arch of sylph in laser limelight, the tulle of her, a target of centerfire— no
music except Pointe knocking into copy paper, fluttering up into the edge of
a circuit board. But in Nevada's desert, past the Citadel gate, a music box
hums by a pile of a dried placenta: a could-be daughter but she had no data—

no Bank of America balance, no search field, no user folder. So the data of her
was unsaved. The data of her needed water. Dear scientist, dear CEO, dear box
humming the Entertainer, her class is ::human:: She is tracing it into the bounds.

SARAH LAIN

Error Log Crushing on an Artist
at Universal Studios

I am the collective software bug. Imagine the erasure of me
as ribbon in your hair, and you: upside down on a roller coaster.
I hold onto your head, blink red through all your flailing.

Imagine the intern who wrote my error log, inventing
for an amusement park owner, the poor intern, believing
for always, the truth of the run job that runs no longer.

Are you thinking of me now, my code through your hair,
while you feed on cotton candy, waiting your turn in line?
Let's leave the roller coaster for good. Take me to your room.

Lay me on the hand-carved hope chest in the corner.
Think of its wood edged into vine and the mahogany man
hunched over something unseen, perhaps a snow globe

waiting to be shaken for the first time, or a light bulb
hungry for its jolt, or a weed before anyone calls it *weed*,
there among never-churned snow. Tie me as globe-bow

and rest my code along your grain. Let's not stay awake.
Pull from yourself the cotton and leather, and dream
of our bus-ride home, where you chose the seat

with stains shaped like strawberries and unbroken foals.
Remember how we rode then, man and ribboned
error code, the cities passing through our mirrored

likeness on the bus windows? At dusk, you lucid-coax
me from my cornered hope. You sing, *come over here.*
I sing, *swing me over your plain and perfect sheets.*

NICOLE ZDEB

Forbidden Monologue

After *Forbidden Music* by Louise Gluck

After lights dim and actors find their spots and the audience feels the embryonic dark and the child actor leaves the stage until tomorrow's performance having said his lines with winning squeak, there comes a scene called the *forbidden monologue* because it cannot, the dramaturg specified during rehearsals, be spoken. Therefore, they never rehearsed it, skipping over it like demanding stage directions.

Yet it *must* be spoken because it has been written.

The lead actress wants very badly to say those words. She can feel them jostling at the base of her throat. She sees them nightly as she sinks into a melatonin-laced fugue. Tonight, the director decides it will be included. He is young. He wants to make his mark. Or he is old. He wants to make his legacy. He tells the lead actress this in that twilight just before curtain. The other actors and stage manager do not know. They are collectively peeved when she veers off script. It is destabilizing and selfish. The child actor floating in the wings sees something he has never seen before. *Who am I?*, he wonders, watching the actress who plays his mother swell and transform. He repeats the question, holding his hands in front of him in the gathered light. *Who am I now?*

MICHAEL PETERS

sassafracas by Suzanne Mercury, ("Xerolage 69," Xexoxical Editions, 2018)

Clocking in at number 69 in the Xerolage series published by the polyartist mIEKAL aND's Xexoxical Editions comes a stunning booklet of visual poetry by Suzanne Mercury. Past Xerolages have featured some esteemed figures of the visual poetic world—historical figures such as Bern Porter and Bob Cobbing, as well as established active figures like Michael Basinski, John M. Bennett, Geof Huth, Clemente Padin, Gustave Morin, Scott Helmes, K.S. Ernst & Sheila Murphy, and Nico Vassilakis, to name just a few of the earlier 68. [Note: Since the publication of Mercury's Xerolage 69, cris cheek has appeared at number 70.] O Parnassus! Part the clouds to clear some head room, and make way for Mercury!

To begin, the full color images are pleasing to engage on flat paper. But Mercury says her poems are "glass poems." So to all the visual poetic typesetters typesetting traditional poems in Photoshop™ in layers of pretty backgrounds, take note that Mercury is actually putting these words on glass. This kind of sensuality is rare in these overly digital days, no? Attempts at description will never completely grant visual poetic work like Mercury's—or the work of past Xerolagists one through 69, for that matter—the attention to detail and nuance it deserves, a description noting the materials might help an un-informed reader understand the nature of this kind of work, and at the same time, illuminate the worthy characteristics for those who recognize the names above and understand the current field of visual poetic practitioners. And what we have here too in addition to noting the materials via description, is the possibility of exposing the circuitry of composition and potential performance.

So, let's proceed even deeper into the *sassafracas*. As pure photos unto themselves, they still kick the work of shallow experimentation in the ass because they exceed the element of mere digital eye candy when you remember these "haptic poems," as she also calls them in her brief introduction to them, are images of physical poems. That is, they are pictures of physical poems: Words put on glass. Mercury does not reveal all of the secrets to her process in her brief introduction, but let us note the words she's using. Mercury says these words *began* as "pwoermds," specifically, which is a term coined by Geof Huth. [See one of Huth's definitions of his neologism: http://dirt-zine.blogspot.com/2006/10/essay-geof-huth-art-of-pwoermds.html.] For example,

Metaphosphor

Aspholdelerium

Melonight …

et cetera. But other words and titles in *sassafracas* don't always play this game either. Got it?

But what's cool is that there's a duality to Mercury's take on the Huthian "pwoermd," that like Huth's word itself, defies the more sound-based semantics of a portmanteau words because a "pwoermd" is/are the words *poem* and *word* folded together (Huth's words paraphrased from an older definition), and as he says, not so much for the air—that is, to be spoken—as they are to be seen. I don't want to engage in a polemic labeling game of definitions, as they too are like opinions, and everybody has them. But I do want to assure you that Mercury is true to this strange visual cementing Huth speaks of, let alone the processes of semantic defiance and intervention of visual literature. And yet she defies Huth's definition too. Why? *Because* these words are on glass, they really *are* meant for the air—but in a silent way. To get this, you have to imagine Mercury holding her work up to sunlit windows or a small desk lamp, burning in a polar vortex'd night. Or maybe you can see Suzanne walking around in her yard—or in the woods—with these sheets of glass that have words on them. Ultimately, she'd be looking at them and through them at the same time, and yet none of these poems would ever be the exactly the same. That's because the environment too would be changing from second to second. [Insert your own system of measuring time here, if you don't prefer seconds.]

So, with environmental interdependence, these poems become ephemeral objects in a vein adjacent to K.S. Ernst's beautiful "object poems," and at the same time, can be played with and documented in all kinds of ways that leads one to deeper understanding. I can't help but think of Robert Smithson's Yucatan Mirror Displacements. Mercury's poems are both airy *and* concrete, glass *and* haptic. Mercury's words *can* hang in the air, so to speak, thanks to the glass, and because of their defiant dualities at a number of levels, they undo the kind of Saussurean circuitry that satiates those addicted to traditional semantics. Got me? *Sassafracas* fucks that all up.

Thus, it's from this dual position in these haptic-glass poems that the circuitry of Mercury's *sassafracas* could—in its own unique ways—always go in at least two directions: **1.)** back out into an ever-changing environment of light, shadow, and landscape, et al, as well as back in **2.)** where our psychogeographical selves are trapped—only momentarily in our immediate interface with the paper of the Xerolage booklet—yet wildly satiated by its poetic delights. Mercury herself says,

I love glass because it is inherently responsive. Lively and reflective by nature, it participates in the environment. It doesn't exclude the world around it. It can't help itself. It fits these pwoermds because they too invite participation, never settling on meaning.

So, Mercury knows the other side of this poetic experience, (direction 1), but we were not and cannot ever have been there with her. What we do get, however, is a different kind of knowing: A delicious, residual documentation that is much more than a pretty backdrop with strange words layered across it in Photoshop™ because what's thrilling for us is the sort of potential here for something like an ecological materialism. Especially if we begin to contemplate the potentially illuminating schematics of *sassafracas*, which is what I'm trying to reveal here, for the schematics of *sassafracas* stimulates a multitude of possible directions that works like Mercury's can take—directions both within and beyond the four rounded corners of North, South, East, and West, which could be as real as it could be delightful.

And then too, if we go in the other direction (direction 2), *sassafracas* is pure document, a work about the work in both images and words, where even the list of materials becomes something akin to art catalog poetry:

Fuchsia variation, dichroic glass with raindrops, hands, and houseplants

Cobalt variation, dichroic glass against yew tree reflecting sky and tree branches

Honeycomb apple variation, dichroic glass against steel with gold and glass dust halo

Got it? It's a materialistic document of what went down in the picture. How many of these poems could be made? How many forever lost?

Okay, I might be a sucker for killer poetic titles of artworks in galleries and museums, as well as the list of materials that comprise the work, but anyone who enjoys the stimulation of words that fly us in and out of contexts will know what I mean, for there is a kind of poetry to "the bride stripped bare of her bachelors," as well as visual delights in photos of shattered glasswork covered in dust, let alone the real work of art itself. *Sassafracas* is an inventive poetic catalog that illuminates potentials and documents reality, but one needs to read Mercury slowly to visualize these reflective abstractions at play. Doing so will provide simple abstract delights, as much as it will point to things we can haptically call real—let alone the means to do it. Mercury is a mysterious journalist working just within and just beyond the fourth estate. And *sassafracas* is full color testament that words in an era of "fake news"—with all its brutal and dismal dualities—could take us somewhere both real and delightful. So, good citizens, we need to think-through-it schematically, or visually, that is, to see-it-through, floating the necessary words into the air where we need them least—or, the most.

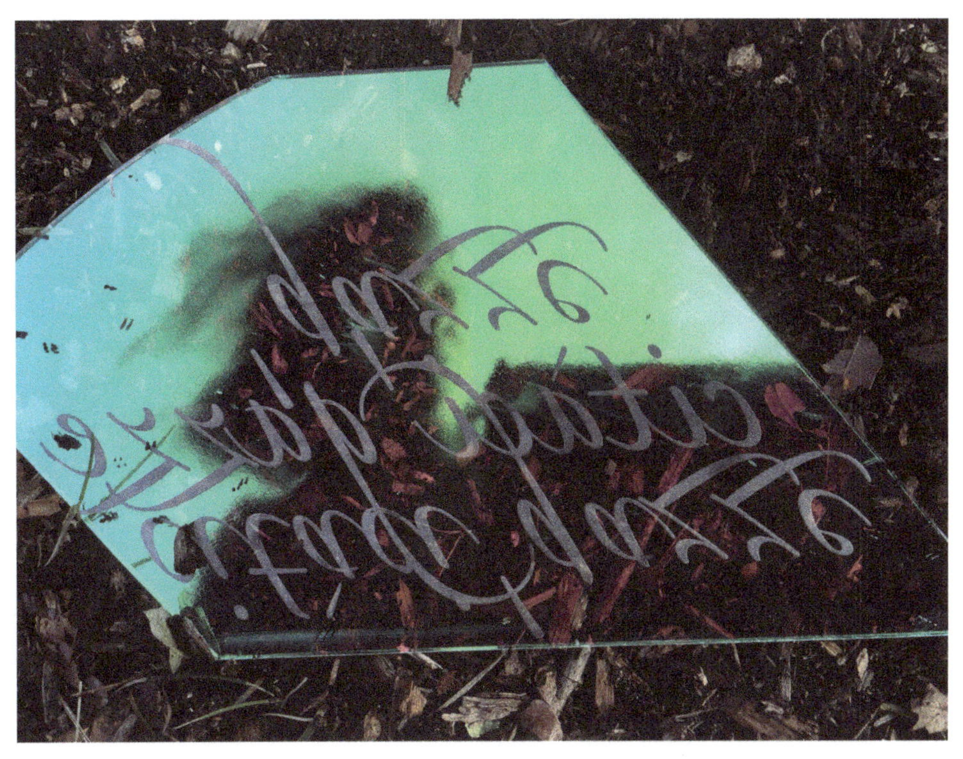

SUZANNE MERCURY

citàci'gázze, 2018. Variation in cerulean and jade, dichroic glass on
earth reflecting sky with self-portrait.

JENIFER DEBELLIS

Natural Instincts

She knows she will get wet today & this doesn't deter her
morning games. Since she's chased away the blue heron,
she hides in the knee-high arrow arum & watches the cattails

& reed grass like the hobby hunter she's become. Moments ago
she nibbled the dry food in her dish with disinterest, scratched
the back door to go out, then slinked to the marsh outskirts—

a kindred image of her panther ancestors. Above grass blades
her head bobs in mimicry of her prey. Missed dive after dive
brings her back to the patio without a win, her black fur spiked

on end. She circles my ankles as I drain my coffee. Her purrs
are in mutual understanding, not defeat. Last week she found
a bunny nest, left one's ears, guts & buns on the stoop as a prize

for me to find. The next day, I ruined her fun when I rescued
the newest bunny—still alive—she brought home. We fought
for hours. She'd re-catch the dazed little thing & I'd pry it free.

That night she forgave me my trespasses with neck kisses
& rumbled bdddaaas, bdddaaas. The next morning, as I sipped
coffee, I watched a red-tailed hawk ascend the blue spruce,

Douglas fir & white pine tree line. Its heavy wing beats
labored against the writhing bunny seized in its curved beak.

SEKYO NAM HAINES

Like a Rising Full Moon
Lyric moment: from Rilke

He is lying there
Motionless,
drifting in and out.

a feeling, a sharp twinge,
arises from his loin,
a pleasant shudder moving up
through his torso to his tongue—

a taste of lemon-buttered artichoke's heart
or, the smell of dried squid—

His head goes blank.
A rush of dark waves—
an oceanic throb floods his body,
which slowly subsides
into a tiny obsidian drop inside his head.

From it, a face,
a face of woman smiling □
rising like a full moon,
filling up the entire inside his head—

A peony bloom
in the depth of his own garden.

JONATHAN AIBEL

Darksomeness

street-light shadows
katakana on the bed
and the little cat slips in,

crouches on the sleeping one,
so soft-footed as to rouse
no more than a skiff of breath.

I stroke her arcuated back,
a feline favor not allowed
by day. The world arranges itself

around my beloved: mattress,
blankets, spiderwebs, nettles,
and this, my form.

JOEY GOULD

Last Meal

I sliced & my friend
considered homelessness.
It was too much on my summer

pay. I gave him two days—
my studio had no doors
& I was used to being

alone. It was a dark
red marbled delight,
New York strip, splayed

& ready to sear. Also,
my father was near-
ly dead & for sure

I needed to grieve,
could I be a father
to anyone else?

On my couch I don't know
if he cried. I was chopping
carrots into jagged coins

& he laughingly named it
his Last Supper. I am no Father,
& he, no Son.

The merlot from my father's
last business deal? I dripped
it into the pan at the end.

He turned into script
resembling Arabic:
beautiful lines & dots

I can't read. I mean
my steak-savoring friend.
I searched for him

on Facebook so I should know.
Maybe he never ate again,
went two dimensional

or gave up on social
media. I applaud that
from five exits down

the turnpike, somewhere
I don't have to try
to cook him any food.

I am no father & watching him
drive away that night
I felt too much like one

to ever want to see him again.

JOEY GOULD

Idiom

Another day in Paradise
The damn light flickering in the breezeway
again, all the nephews in dinosaur costumes
knocking at front doors in unison
when all uncles just put the action movies in.
Stagger back to the couch & next thing you know
the alarm is doing whatever annoying thing
you ask, no, beg of it each—call it dawnish,
reach for the comfort of a travel mug.
God, it's just coffee, Jane. Stopped at that light
that takes for-ev-er, after two hours you watch
a church girl take a violin from a case, wishing you were
that terrific a kid, or holy enough, something.
She sees you watching her, I'll bet she'd
play if you pled for gospel. At work the apples
are bent, we're out of left-handed pickles & crystallized
ginger. The pallet lopsided, deli kicking the kombucha
off. Everyone asks for the lefty pickles. Suffer it for a buck,
for a nephew-hug & the cool drip of a Dino Egg
brand plumcot in that corner of the backroom
the camera can't catch. The pallet jack catches
every case, stacked & stacked & stacked in a cross-hatch
for weight stability. The customers come past
& everything is theirs if they want it, if they'll
take it home with them to their veloci-nephews,
who peel them, roaring, bite in, it's a bloodbath,
the pulp everywhere. Uncle, down the hall,
screws in a new bulb. *There*, he says, *perfect.*

Starfish

—for my friend, Mani

The arms of starfish have
little eye-dots at their tips
to take in the salt-ache of the sea,
the light and dark of shoals.
Contrast is all they see
like my friend, whose

vision has gone backwards
through the years until
the apartment building
behind his eyes is blanketed
with blackout. Photons
and wavelength give way

to iambs and pentameter.
For starfish touch is more
primal than sight. Sometimes
when we talk, I'll put
my hand on Mani's shoulder,
so he can feel I'm listening.

BARBARA HELFGOTT-HYETT

The River *Dure*

I have come to suffer
her bark-streaked world
where toads call out
in the riverdark, all that
effort to find one another
waiting wetly on river stones.

The Dure renews itself by that
sound and time takes itself
seriously. I will stay and be
made of staying. Let the river.
Let the cold. There is too much
world to fail. I will sleep the night,

glad to be sleeping, glad to wake
as myself, like always, like never
before. No whispers. No breath
upon my neck; Let love wait
like an umbrella in its stand—

There may be no need.

Chell Navarro

Poem Made Long After the Situation
-Drawing No. 13, 1915

It was more about the dream
of falling.

My foot raised in the air
to step off,

the fright of the day,

standing on an edge
at Palo Duro.

With a walking stick in hand
to steady—

I spotted a long line of cows,
they looked

like widow's
lace on the canyon trail below.

CINDY VEACH

Mary Ayer Parker
Hanged, September 22, 1692

It is written that her touch alone
recovered the afflicted out of their fits.

And there was that black hog,
or some Evill thing not a Reall hog,

that chased home old man Westgate,
open-mouthed, as if it—*would have*

devoured me att that Instant. He said,
he had determined in his mind,

it was Goody Parker.
Also, William Barker Jr. confessed

she *went w'th him to Afflict Martha Sprague*
and that she *rod upon a pole*

and was baptized at 5 Mile pond—
But to this day there's speculation

that the teenage girls who accused her
meant another Mary Parker—

distemper of the mind Mary Stevens Parker
or sister-in-law Mary Markstone Parker

or possibly niece Mary Parker
but, most likely, the scandalous

twice-convicted of fornication
and mother of an illegitimate child

Mary Parker of Salem Town
instead of the hanged Mary Ayer Parker—

Still, Mary, Mary, Mary, Mary or Mary
equals innocent times five.

Quotes (in italics) and inspiration from Salem Witch Trials Documentary
Archive and Transcription Project. http://salem.lib.virginia.edu/texts/tei/
swp?div_id=n98; The Untold Story of Mary Ayer Parker: Gossip and Confu-
sion in 1692, by Jacqueline Kelly, Salem Witch Trials Documentary Archive
and Transcription Project.

MARY ANN HONAKER

The Light Chain

How we filled the room
with ourselves until it was a pool
sloshing with mockery and howls.
We were loud and brash and laughed a lot.

After we dimmed a bit, at last,
an irritating buzz tapped
out of the background into focus,
punctuated with fleshy thumps,

and looking up, we saw the eight
fat flies bumper-carring the bulb,
circling it as we would a twigfire,
raging, drunk with brightness.

When you took off your shoe,
and stood on your chair,
you still had to leap
to smash them.

We laughed, of course,
until Phillip said, you're making a mess,
and we all agreed you should come down.

But you refused, swearing;
slavering in a Bacchic trance,
you crushed the last of the little beasts.

After this it rolls out, film from a tin:
you beating that boy who never wronged you:
three fast flash jabs, glare of your teeth,

him falling in a roar that either came
from your mouth or echoed out
from my own;

slapping your girlfriend to the graveyard's
ground for pissing on a grave,
and finally, of course, turning on me.

I pull the light-chain on this night.
The blood lingers on the lambent white.

     MARY ANN HONAKER

KONNER JEBB

Your Dad's Death Everywhere

Chopping trees in your eyes. Your eyes,
I see him nestled there within this house
he built, hoarded beneath tears
unreleased in ceiling lamps.
He's in every wall, sick
asleep in the guest room we stay in,
motionless on these bathroom tiles☐
pearl pink, the bedroom you hide in
and your lie, "Its fine"
when the ambulance arrives.

HEATHER HUGHES

My Tarantella by Jennifer Martelli
(Bordighera Press, 2018, $10)

Maybe you never heard of her. Maybe you barely heard of her. Maybe you heard her name somewhere, you're sure it rings a bell, but you can't put your finger on why, and you don't search out any of the details. Maybe you type her name and see the Wiki summary and think, "oh, yeah, her." And move on with your day. Maybe you heard all about her all the time—her, or any other girl or woman like her, brutalized at random and held up as an anti-example—and wished you hadn't, wished the stray misfortune of a total stranger weren't used by people who love you to say that somehow a woman living her life on her own terms deserves what she got, didn't do enough to avoid trouble, so don't be her, never be her. Maybe, like the speaker in the poem "Astronomers Added the Unicorn to the Orion Constellation Family for Completeness", you are walking around the North End in Boston, the Italian neighborhood, Italian-I and Italian friends, talking about her, about how you can't stop thinking and writing about her: "I asked my friends, *How do you pronounce her name?* Olivia said, *Well, we'd say Gen-Oh-Vay-Zee.* Laurette said, *Maybe you're writing about her because she wasn't heard, or she was heard and not listened to.*"

There is a dance in turning the pages of Jennifer Martelli's second book *My Tarantella.* Not precisely the folk dance referenced in the book's title, but not precisely not, either. Martelli's unflinching collection loops and whirls around the murder of Kitty Genovese. In the book's notes, Martelli writes "I conflated aspects of Kitty Genovese's story as an Italian-American woman with my own, wove some of my own memories with her story." What Martelli does is much more than conflating implies. This is not, overall, a collection of persona poems, not an attempt to inhabit Kitty Genovese's life. That would simply be a different book. Instead *My Tarantella* enacts a dialog between a living Italian-American woman and a dead one, exposing the joys and violences inherited from Italian tradition, American history, patriarchy, and pop culture. As Martelli writes in the poem "Dear Kitty,":

> "I am breaking my own rule talking to the dead for the sake of the living. I want to imply a sense of intimacy between us. I want witness and eavesdroppers. I don't believe in consciousness after death. I believe you are gone. But I found a Kodak of me in front of my aluminum Christmas tree the Advent after you died: my hair, short and black like yours in the mug shot, and my cousin in her pink Danskin had your bow and arrow eyebrows."

The intimacy crops up throughout the collection, repetitions echolocating like the bats that appear sporadically throughout. Martelli returns again and again in various ways to how the book's speaker identifies intimately with Kitty Genovese; one such powerful example being the "short black hair like yours" that crops up consistently. In "Pomona Street", the book's narrator is a very young girl fixating on her hair, the "nape with its little V," who "begged not to have it shorn into a pixie." Here Martelli fuses a scene from an Italian-American beauty salon, echoes back to the similarities between the I and Genovese, calls up the expectations and disappointments and kinships that surround not only a particular cultural upbringing and a particular era, but also the fact of moving through American patriarchy in a woman's body and the ways in which choice and self-ownership are circumscribed. The last four lines of "Pomona Street" underscore this:

> "After, to stop my crying, Quinn the bookie
> gave me something sweet on a stick.
> I asked for green but I got red. I asked
> for my mother, but got my aunt."

In Martelli's sure hands, the scene stays light, delicately humorous—it's only a haircut—but because *My Tarantella* contains numerous such strong image echoes, there's trust built up that allows the reader to hear and participate and connect the dots.

Martelli adroitly choreographs time and place throughout the collection, using carefully rendered particulars and poem titles to keep the reader situated despite significant leaps along the way. These details not only locate the reader, they put intimate specifics of women's lives in conversation with American history writ large. A striking instance is the poem "After JFK's Assassination, Things Got Really Bad." The title immediately situates the reader, but simultaneously allows Martelli to move effortlessly through time with that anchor point established. In the first line, a question is posed—"*Why are you writing about her?*"—which swings from 1963 (not-so-coincidentally a moment when both the author and Genovese were alive) to the 2010s. Then the poem jumps back to the scene of Genovese's murder in 1964, but seen through the lens of the speaker's present-day recollection of her own youth: "Kitty Genovese was / menstruating that night, the Kotex was held in place with the garter straps, / how my mother showed me." The menstrual pad conveys the image of blood and violation, yes, but Martelli takes the detail further. With that private and taboo yet absolutely commonplace product, she marks the utility of the garter belt, its functionality, at a particular historical moment that overlaps with the assassination of JFK. Again, the author leaves some of the work to the reader, allows these elements to speak to one another across time and space and resonate for the reader beyond the page, to hear the everyday voice of a woman against the backdrop of a pivotal American political crisis. Or take, as another instance of simple details conveying how contemporary national emergency speaks to Genovese's personal tragedy, these lines from part 1 and part 3 of "Anniversary": "I've thought of Kitty Genovese for a long time: her mouth" and "Hilary's mouth was a red slash. / I saw a woman wearing a silk-screen t-shirt: *Trump that bitch.* So I knew it was over." The juxtapositions and echoes of intentionally chosen observations in these lines suggest a complex understanding of how American patriarchy fails women, how society can often fall short of a person's hopes.

There's more to say. I could go on and on. The work invites introspection and questioning that's maybe better explored in dialog. *My Tarantella* is a rewarding poetry book that, for all its trappings of speaking to the dead, never loses sight of the present moment or entwined the intimate is with cultural and social and national concerns. Martelli's writing speaks powerfully to the living and asks that we not forget how close the past is. In "Fatal Mouths" she writes:

> "If there is a God, His indifference has settled deep
>   within
> my ribcaged country. Last night, on television, I saw
>   a woman scrubbed
> of makeup give a speech. I read about a woman who
>   screamed
> but no one came."

JENNIFER MARTELLI

Two Cats Dilate, Warning & Wanting

The month of August circles around itself, circles my whole house.

Nothing can move, not one us, not my blue impatiens cramped & fat

in their black cone baskets hanging from the porch. When I stuck three fingers

deep down in dirt (repetitively for the tiny roots) back in May

I think I was happy, I think I wanted it to be warmer right then

yes, I'm sure I was wanting something, because that is my hollow nature.

I'd painted these baskets black, sprayed the oil-based paint from a small can

I shook just to hear the bead: I wanted two tornados hanging down

from my front porch, I wanted two plague masks, two crows' beaks
    with tangled vines—

On the steaming hot top, two cats dilate warning & wanting & wide-

eyed, flat-eared. They turn themselves into thick low snakes, hiss
    from their long guts.

CAROL HOBBS

On TV, Two Girls Go Missing

Because the sparrow's song is sometimes confused
with a child's small voice calling
mother
through the doorway, through the open window,
I reorganize the muscles of my lips
into a small knot, slip
out into the neighborhoods to search the trees,
the disquiet, lift of air.

Remaining Turns

Dig the mulched center from our felled oak.
I'll set ferns in the hollow, be with you
through these remaining turns. We brush leaves
from a channel in descending sludge,
redirect what we can. Mud skid under shoes

splashed brown, the drop from a nose
that's not a tear. Darkening, birds call
as we roll a blue tarp filled with leaves –
soiled elbows in need of washing.
Through rippled glass it all looks better –

bent and toweling you tell me,
You'll always be my fleshy blur. I show off,
a clear steam circle of growing sex
in obscuring showers, a chamber door,
a leaded window above the tub.

SANDY WEISMAN

Matins

I begin to dream. My mind as big
as the universe, empty, so easy
to travel unballasted through space.

Nothing solid. I pass my self sitting
on the window seat, reading mysteries.

I pass my father and all the boys I've ever loved,
still boys, pulling me very fast
in a red wagon around the corners on my street.

I pass my mother dying, peaceful finally.
Soft whispers from the universe□
I am inside the hour glass.

MATTHEW SISSON

Aunt Camille Cut Off Her Hand

chopping escarole
for her chicken escarole soup.

Be more careful in the future,
said the hand wagging a finger, interrupting
my aunt's lecture on Bruno Bettelheim's
"Uses of Enchantment." It jumped off
the butcher-block and began flying
around the room. Zucchini, my aunt's
Dachshund we call "Zook, Zook," howling.

Come back here! said my aunt.

*No, you are tone deaf, and I
have always wanted to play
the piano.*

But we don't even have a piano.

I know that, the hand said
unsurprised.

My aunt fell silent as a clock tower.

The hand performed one last barrel roll,
then flew out the window
without waving good-bye.

My parents spend a great deal of time
traveling. My sister and I are sent to
Aunt Camille. She loves us.

MARIA SEBASTIAN

Ode to the House Dress

And so even the children of hard-to-like mothers
find secret comfort in house dresses
reminiscent of those Mom wore to lean out
her warning-window for dinner reminders

the polyester kind never show signs
of opening pickle jars or beer bottles
lace trim frames housework as joyful
from cupboards to carpets to catnaps

few can tell when I pair one with heels
and wear it to work where students
may not recognize a house dress
until projected like a pop-culture skylight

peeking into kitchens of sitcom sweeties
and no matter our feminist findings
we miss our hovering TV honeys
who always fixed us a bite to eat

or a one-liner ready-to-serve hot or cold
ghetto-gowns glow in city courtyards
lean over laundry lines by Chinese tea houses
in floral patterns of long-gone gardens

grouped by color and hanging wall to wall
in Salvation Armies across America
house dresses wait like surrogate mothers
waving flags of forgiveness for everyone

WINONA'S WAIL
After winona la duke

on the late great plains
we've turned native grass—
that wants no water from pipes—
upside down

two hundred plush species
turned upside down

districts and sections and plots
zones and tracts and parcels
turned upside down
to grow   one kind   of cattlegrass
addicted to pipe water

      consider buffalo   of solid thunder hooves
      and lightning eyes
      buffalo   not afraid to walk into storms

      buffalo   evolved by great plains
      not afraid   to plow under snow
      to feed on grass   beneath

      but one dead winter
      eleven hundred shot by cattle keepers
      for crossing out of frozen yellowstone
      eleven hundred shot on slopes   looking for grass
      lower down

fattened cattle run from storms
need to be watered
need to be drugged
need to be fed   that one captive grass

outside denver   late one day   in mad downpour
whole cattle families panic and run   into flooded gullies
following the ones in front
whole cattle families panic and die   by thousands

under great plains   corporate pumps
levitate ancient ground water away
as sweet oglala aquifer
drops four feet   per year
recharges one-half inch   per year

sweet oglala elixir
spills out for cattle and their grass
(and we beasts who eat them)

in furnished vertical tree stumps
on prairie edge
managers   gather under artificial light
invoke bottom-line gods
applaud the latest sins in grass genetics

managers   gather to sing
from chemical fertilizer hymnals
sing until their eyes water
like sweet oglala aquifer

      out on dusty domains
      in blanket-wrapped sweat lodges
      warriors meet in absolute dark
      to pray for buffalo nation
      to chant for water spirit
      for sacred grasses
      for rock and tree cousins

      in absolute dark
      warriors meet to wail
      for ranchers' bullets
      to rot in their chambers

RIKKI SANTER

Pop Tart Confidential

They came in blank boxes,
serial numbers their only moniker.
Week after week, toast or cereal
was banned in my house
until we tangoed with every single
experimental version of those
sweet-filled rectangles.
We were a test family then,
quantifying our tongues on bubbled,
poker-faced ballots
and now I am a test patient
waiting for a surgical biopsy
and the godding that follows
for right results—that perfect
strawberry jam to fill me.

Three a.m. and I itch all over
with the nooks and crannies
of how well will this episode finish?
I take refuge on the living room couch
spare my generous husband
a bit more fretting. In candlelight
on the coffee table a magazine cover
greets me: *50 Things to Eat
Before You Die* which gets me snickering
then thinking about the back
of Jerry Seinfeld's head "blowing right off"
when he was a 60s kid like me
first hearing the name of this pastry.

So sweet Mother and Poppa Tart,
even though you are long gone, I need
you now to shepherd me. Speedway
probably open at this hour.
I'm needing a family reunion

Quiz on Love Proem

Name_________________________
Your One (or two) True Love(s)___________________________

1. If Love is to anaphylactic shock as Love is to meeting, then Love is to lunchbox as Love is to ____________________.

a. Is that a thing? Does it got that swing? Shh bop, shebop. b. The heart is the transceiver and receiver of all things, like a spiritual biological transistor radio, so that even during storms, you can almost hear some body some place. c. cheeseburger. d. Look at how ugly my calf muscles are. I'm fat. My hair isn't straight enough, black enough, perfect enough, white enough, shiny. Who wants "I"s like mine?

1. Three things remain: faith, hope, and _________________.

 a. Love, love, love: all you need is love. (b. Is love a tender thing? Is it too rough? They tried to bury us. They didn't know we were seeds.) c. The Lake of Fire. Sheol. Eternal Separation from God. Jahannam. Nothingness. d. As a child, I believed I needed to be something to be lovable. I, my self, wasn't enough. My unlovable parts I hid, believing they were the reasons why I wasn't lovable. Did you? Do you?

1. The following diagram illustrates how love, a real thing, grows from first sight to the last action before dying.

1. How does a murderer love? How is love murder? How does a briar love? How is love briaring? How does a leader love? How is love leading? How does a chef love? How is love cheffing? How does a lover ask too many questions? How is love questioning?

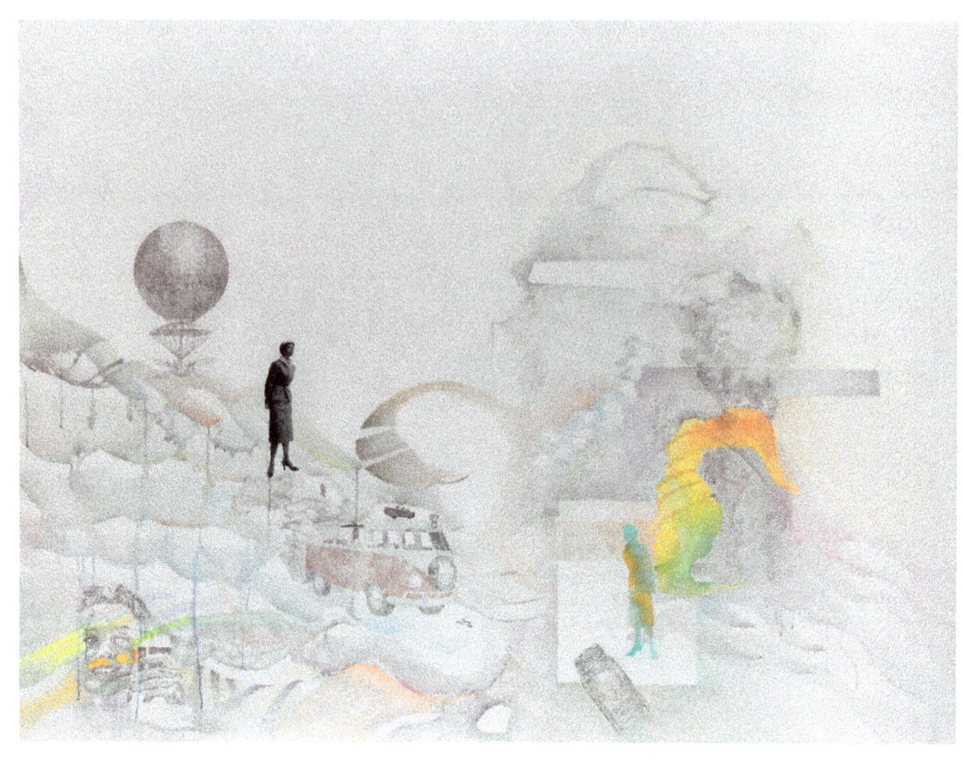

ALEXIS AVLAMIS
LISTENING TO THE BEATLES

EILEEN CLEARY

The World is My Rival by **Charlotte Seley**
(Spuyten Duyvil, 2018, $15)

Have you ever been certain of something, then not so sure?

The lyrical speakers in *The World is My Rival* might have initially sided with Aristotle and agreed that barnacles spontaneously generate from wood. However, they would just as likely pick up Pasteur's goose-necked flask and debunk that myth. These speakers are convinced that "clouds aren't real," but "don't know what it means to live in a cloud." It's this lyrical curiosity that delights the reader in this collection brimming with what speakers believe, even as they question their beliefs.

We are, as always, in a time of significant change and dynamic landscape. We find ourselves at once on fire and frozen, in this earth rich in resources and diminishing. Perhaps, like Seley, we ask whether upturned sea shells "promote growth or death." These poems resonate in their desire to explore understandings: the yin and yang, the interconnections of our human-made environments and the natural world, to know our inner selves even as we wonder how people see us "from afar."

Of course, Seley also explores the speaker's interior and relationships, what they know and don't know of love.

And in this world, where so many of us are asea, is it any wonder Seley "forgot" she was "suspended in water?" Is it surprising that she seeks instead "to be ocean?" That would be a vaster body, one less easily drowned, burned or frozen.

Becoming the ocean would allow what these poems seek: limitless discovery.

DAVID SOMERSET

Aleppo

"—and where they made a desert, they called it peace." Tacitus

What about Aleppo? the candidate asks.

I think of hands torn trying to rescue
children from bombed building carcasses
and this dark juggernaut of insanity.

War and all war means, as terrible
as a genocide, as a massacre, as a rape
between commercial breaks.

MANI IYER

Driving North through New England

What my retinas cannot
capture, my wife captures.

Leaves
dazzle and purple.

She has nothing to add
for miles, miles.

I picture a pale grey
not-much-to-look-at nakedness,
birches standing solemn—

My wife startles me, tells me
a bride is driving this sky blue
car in the left lane, radiant.

MANI IYER

Dance of Existence

Dressed in the dazzle of sequins
and a thousand rainbows,
the Goddess dances to a silent score
she alone knows.

Out of the throbbing: I appear,
I linger, I disappear.
Not just me, but the cloud
and the wind and the wave,
the butterfly and the whale,
the dandelion and the sequoia,
the loon and her cry.

She lifts her foot, sways her hand,
twists her torso, pirouettes.
In tune with her
I am the dancer,
I am the dance,
I am the dancing.

Dr. Ansari Road

Right next to the roadside shrine
of Lakshmi, goddess of prosperity,
I expect him: a tattered heap
of flesh, waving
flies off his bruised face
with the stump of one hand, the other
on his begging bowl.

The copper bowl brims with coins
dropped by they who hurry away
before he blesses them.
Still, he smiles,
his arms raised in a *namasté*.

I never see his legs—
he has none.
Like clockwork he shows up
on his roller board,
monsoons never a damper.

When he does keel over,
disinfected air will greet me,
a day before another
leprous beggar appears
with bowl and board, ready
to fatten the flies.

ANTHONY G. AMSTERDAM

For an Orchard Suicide

Yours was not the world's end.
You thought it was, but when you'd built
your gallows of an apple tree,
a gold and onyx bee
buzzed about your dead hand
languidly.

Before the migrant workers came,
the tree had seen
snows, rains, rains,
rivulets of silt
and blooms.

Until a hump-backed beggar woman, all alone beneath
    a crescent moon,
plucked you down still green
and took you home and
fed a healthy infant your ripe milk.

FRANCIS LUNNEY

Montana

White wooden crosses appear along the two-
lane highway, cluttered with flowers,

sheltered from rain by plastic grottoes,
a cross with its own Mary, eyes painted blue,

hands extended for someone she'll never know.
Near Browning, a cross leans hard into the wind

like a man stumbling across the sidewalk
towards the day's first drink.

KATHY NILSSON

Incontinent Nostalgia

New clouds glided effortlessly along
and big furry canines were on the loose.
We headed outside into many little guillotines.
When I looked down, blood matched my shoes.

I thought about my bean plant in school
and at night I thought about the past——
a secluded spot in the woods where kids could
last until found by mushroom hunters in spring.

Earth wasn't so crowded then—— and yet everyone
was still alive. Night dawned innocently on summer
evenings. A whistle called us to come home.
The sun set without riffling a child's hair.

LISA RUA-WARE

COD

My father places the dried fish in a basin of water
watches over the cod for days, nurses the flesh.
changes the watery bandage where sea and salt
shed like dead skin and my father
carefully rinses the pieces,
washes them like baby feet, plump
for the bubbling tide, that can soften and soothe,
that will crumble onto a plate, steaming.

REBECCA HART OLANDER

Cartomancy

The sky is purpled blue, lung
tissue. Flapping the striated
clouds, a band of birds, heading
out of town. Propped over a swath
of solitaire, the suicide king
stares up at me from his perch
on the pile. Some say he evolved
into his pain, the axe head once
shown raised and ready, drawn out
of the picture over time. I think it's
intentional, this self-inflicted wound.
Ruler of hearts, he knew in love
there's always a bushel of pain.

DAVID P. MILLER

What God Knows

A golden shovel, after Jane Hirshfield and Jim Harrison

Leaves turned, not by breeze in general, but by the
exact wind of a gone moment, now dissolved across dead
ailanthus twigs and my demurely flaking skin. And do
you consider how much of dust is made of fallen skin? It's not
only that we return to dust. We are dust. Much as we want
our brooms to cleanse the floor, the persistent scatter is us.
Now reconsider each different breeze. When dead

and merged with the empyrean, perhaps with God
we'll know all zephyrs as the one Zephyr that is.
I'm done with fussing over what God knows. Only
let me seize a dustpan of debris, settle myself on
the morning's sweep-up. The celestial part is God's,
I guess, with spent ailanthus branches left to the side.

Adopt the World

Stop, at last, to examine
the heavy bark.
The branch that leaves
should burst from a sister
throwing open the front door.
Don't turn away.
Kneel where you are.
Count each toe of grass.
Lilacs to your chest,
scent of infant skin.
Dig deep for roots.
Pack dirt under your nails.
Hoard it like birthday cake.

KYLE POTVIN

Chime of Wrens

Take this world,
all its honking, hip hop and hiccups.

Caws and creaks,
talk-show staccato and bugled taps.

Silence the click-clack
of stilettos on stone,

car doors and door knocks,
coffee beans bouncing off the shocked floor.

And please!
Make those honey-sucking bees stop!

Let the kettle grow cold,
the fan stand still.

No more shifting of sand
or petals peeling away from their stem.

Let your mind rise, a chime
of wrens startled from the tree.

CLARISSA ADKINS

Elongation

Thinking of northern places
makes her dizzy lids

want to burrow through the gelid
to the end of skies.

She eyes a precipice,
just a distant cartography.

She pilots her walking,
calculates latitude cracks,

city footpaths—loses count—
a sidewalk must have an end.

She believes northbound concrete
can only lead to Canada, or cold-fish

shades of blue sky, or to splintered piers
stacking surface onto water. She wonders

how land hides its height
in the fog at Saint John's Bay—

why the heedless geese mock her
with winged elation. Why they pocket

into the pulling whip of undertow tide—
still, she moves north—

her cold feet touching the longitude tightrope,
the thinning air rising

like its own balloon—propelling her above glacier—
up and up again, in increments, with the precision of eagles.

She swears, now, this is the end of Earth
and Nova Scotia, where the edges

roll into cotta dough of pine terrain—
the land strands stretching into transparency,

to where wandering boreal
eats snow-covered Taiga.

MICHELLE BROOKS

Tabloid Dreams

I am writing to you from a far-away
place. The future is nowhere in sight.
You won't learn anything new. I'm not
alone – the ghosts whisper into intercoms
at night. There's a suitcase in the hallway
that I keep forgetting to move. Sometimes
the light shines into this darkness, and I read
magazines with pictures of the famous
dead, piles of yesteryear's scandals. None
of this matters anymore. It's always late
afternoon, and I'm always waiting for someone
to come home. A lit cigarette rests on a saucer
that has never been used for anything except ashes.

ACE BOGGESS

Driving Through Kanawha State Forest

Day of a single color
for jealousy &
inexperience—
how it fluffs trees,
taints the pond.

There was sunlight miles ago.
It too has taken jaded tones.

Grace, beside me,
points out weeds,
places she took part in falls &
motorcycle accidents.

I'm not sure what
we've come to see.
Whatever it is
will never be enough.

RENUKA RAGHAVAN

WITHOUT A PLACE

The mens-only room at the night shelter
had no space for personal epiphanies.
Like metal tongued by a torch's fire,
these men welded into one,
their dreams fated by auspicious disasters,
blackened flesh, earned cotton,
sedulous odors, their smug seed.

The women sat on park benches
calling out to pigeons by name,
whispering to each other like a steady drizzle,
making obscure prophecies,
lost in a haze as if searching
for something they had vomited up
that never returned back to the earth.

Together, they shiver like January nights,
in a dreamless sleep around Dupont Circle,
sharing their stories.
A tale for each fold and wrinkle of skin.
A caution for each cut, scar.
Their stories still glow around dark corners,
like cat eyes, like Gatsby's green light, afire.

RENUKA RAGHAVAN

DIORAMA

Mrs. Miller asked with bored eyes for us to pick a country.
Any country. Create a 3-D diorama.
India, not for my heritage,
because I remember when Daddy watched TV last night.
Breaking News: Earthquake hits Northern India.
Nearly 2,000 dead, more than 300,000 missing, injured, displaced.

I paper mâchéd a house inside an old shoe box out of thick
black construction paper,
somewhere along the foothills of the Himalayas, snow-capped
peaks pasted for background.
The walls of the house shook,
floors torn apart, upturned furniture littered the inside,
like when Daddy used to play dollhouse with me
but his hand was too big to fit the tiny rooms.

You can't tell anything is wrong, said Mrs. Miller,
the house looks like any other. But I know.
I know you have to walk to the yard out back,
so I showed her the gnarled swingset,
the plastic tricycle, going through the bottom of the shoebox,
swallowed by earth,
the wooden sandbox blown asunder.

EVE LINN

Model Home

A glacial hive

      all passages   frozen

surfaces slick corners

sharp a door   a peephole   a glass

fisheye   faces   looked at me

we were the *Shape-Me-Family*

Father   Mother   Big Sister   little sister

Father outside on the painted grass   Mother in the tub

      with no water

MARTHA MCCOLLOUGH

Little House in the Forest of Giant Ferns

prequel or aftermath
faint fiddle music
along green aisles

your bones vibrate
to a note bowed on
the deepest string

otherwise only
soft insect hum
clicking carapace

of giant scorpion
or millipede deep
in the shady grove

there was or will
be a prairie a big
wood a creek bank

ghost pa's in the parlor
playing *boil that
cabbage down*

MARTHA MCCOLLOUGH

Well, Now We Are in the Forest of Arden

between sleep
and deepest sleep

comes mending—
thinnest needle

stitching up the map
a series of careful knots

if, then, else:
error creeps in
along the seam

moss and granite
heaped among the pines
here is a way to be lost

we'll follow
ghost light or
milk-white hind

since there is no path
through the steep-folded
back and forth

the pools reflect
strangers' faces

changed & changed
in the uncertain light

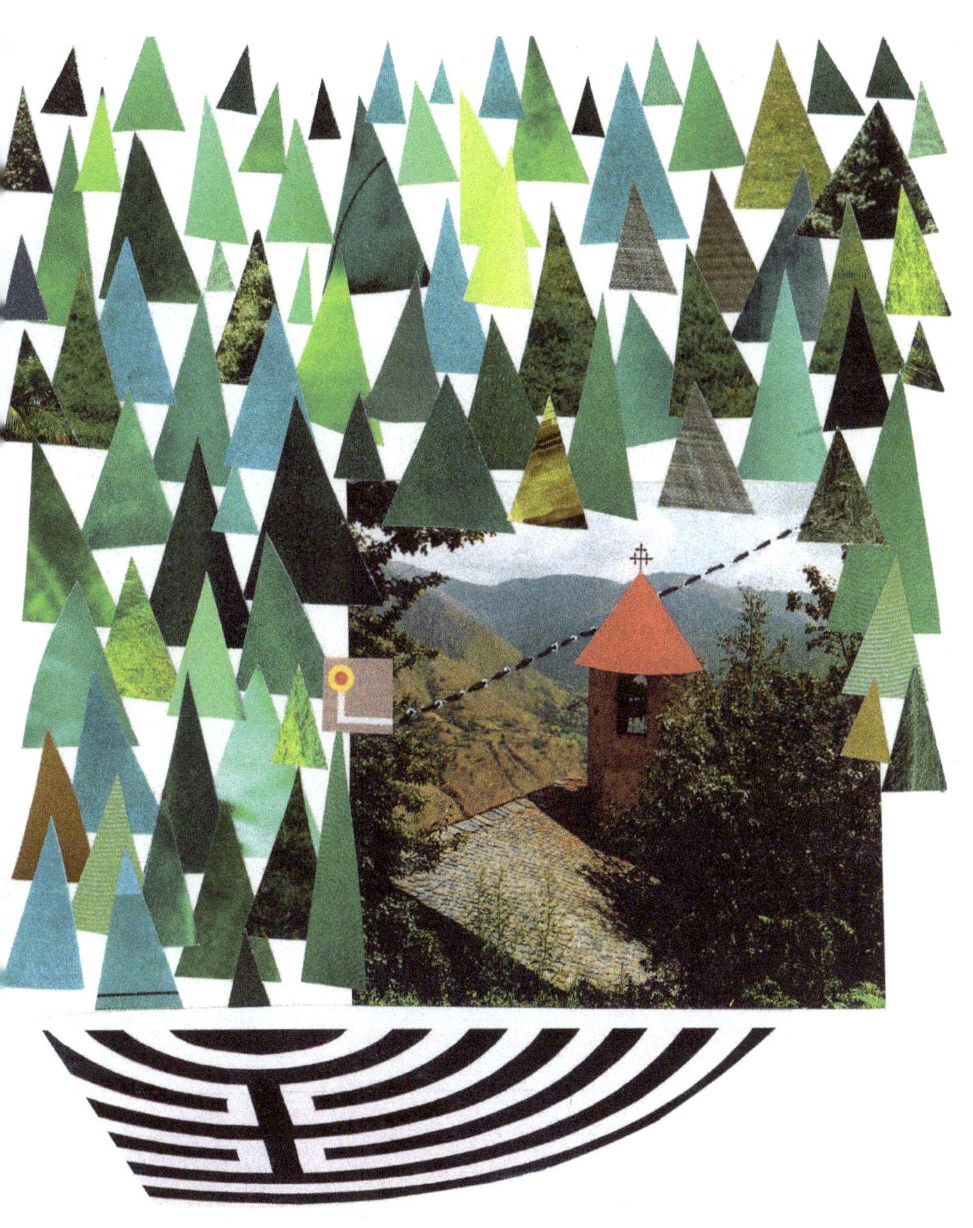

SARAH SLOAT
IN THE PINES

125

M.A. BOWERSOCK

EARLY GRID PLAN, NEW HAVEN

Can you pick me up, under the overpass, past the projects, at the train station, can you give me a ride, my car's been towed to Kimberley Avenue somewhere north of Montowese, can you take me to West Haven for an iced tea, can you tell me once and for all who makes the best pizza pie and how do you get there from here?

Beech leaves, blown across the glue between two pavements, stuck there, and the seams held the marks long after the leaves went away, dirty black scrawlings like moons the years I walked through there yearning for someplace else. Just so, slate walkways in rain, the pounded-in prints of the maple leaves.

She and he exchange descriptions of their desires standing over the goldfish breathing in the grass of the yard. What have we done? We have come back from the late-nite grocery where we bought distilled water and a quart of our own chocolate ice cream and for once there's track on the TV and we

L-O-V-E it.

Out the way of the cotton gin and Winchester Repeating Arms I transposed February into the subjunctive, the past contrary-to-fact. *If I had left that show If I had walked back to my room If I had written down the rainlight If I had settled down to work.* Even my grandmother had it memorized: *Forsan et haec olim meminisse juvabit.*

In a basement kitchen she and I cooked beans and rice with brown sugar we sang blue songs we swapped know-hows, breaths in chamber music and my sense of direction, relying on good features and diminutive looks, best spits. Together we raced through hamburger corner. Together it made us men.

The Oak Street Connector never got built but they tore the houses down anyway. In the seventies. The swath of dry grass, still there. Saddling up, I'd review: this hour plus twelve equals home. This plus seven is familyland number two. Plus one-half, past James Farm Road, is third best but it is close enough. I will take it.

When I was one she was zero minutes from the morning pool and we both heard something under the water and didn't think much of it in the gut-ache of all those sit-ups, the slime and echo of the pooldeck, my housekeys sliding under, to the wavery black lane lines, to the bluest blue again.	Let the art gallery prints pour out their reproach Let some Thursday and Sunday nights drape over a person Let the courtyard swing dangle above its muddy under-puddle Let suicides dream of the GW bridge. On the sidewalks we meet the morning's first cigarette. We will wish we had known them better.	Coming back to Dwight Street in summer, there is still the half-painted house and the smell of marijuana on her sexy girl-friend, still the men in rich-col-ored giant masks who climb all the way down the side of a tower, at night, lit from underneath. I am tired of festivals. My car is gone. It must have been towed again.

M.A. BOWERSOCK

Induction From Strewn Objects: After Columbia

It's easy to speculate. It's easy to be confused.
There is a lot of things laying around in this country.

—Spaceflight Deputy Michael Kostelnik

An egg yolk
unshelled
on an old woman's porch. (Shreveport, La.)

Sheet metal. (Antioch, Calif.)
Orange siding from a powerboat. (Central Florida.)
Burned toast. (Yuma, Ariz.)

A team combing
the woods was led by a local boy
to a Chevy alternator

maybe with him talking the whole
length of the ravine in an inscrutable
pinewoods argot, him

small, a loner, or in it for the publicity,
or innocent, Sylvy leading them the long way
so not to disturb the bird.

He knew the place,
and the blue bleaching sky'd
dropped this there on the vast

plain, where socks, lottery tickets,
lampshades, souvenir visors
were already resting themselves

in its ditches, and who, anyway, could have
found that place for the alternator,
if not the sailing seven?

Eventually found were the 500 pound
nose cone, fins and remains. They plotted
the points across the map:

The outer part of the left wing
began to separate at Waxahachie. Then the right.
East, all the way to the state line.

SEAN THOMAS DOUGHERTY

Dear Editors Who Didn't Send Me
Interesting Rejection Letters

The ones whose imprint never even stayed, little more than the
way a leaf palimpsests the sidewalk after being washed away by
rain.

~

The same language we are told so often in this life: go away.
And we do, and let the words leave us.

~

To you, I want to give you something, say, from the basement
butcher shop, a leg of lamb, a bloody steak. You've done no
damage, you left no mark, you let me escape, or was I recused?

~

And so, I hand you a glass moon of whiskey. A Ferris Wheel
rising over the lake. The dark that rests after the wheat has
been reaped. I send you what the bird feels, as the air first fills
its wings. Even sparrows sing. Not only the rain can fill the
emptiness of two palmed hands.

~

Soon they will ride in his blue Chevrolet and lay on towels
down at the city park that runs along the lake, the sand full of
bottle caps and cigarette butts, they won't care.

~

This isn't an analogy for adolescence, a story told to test, but a
longing before loss.

~

To return to a moment before he left, and became an obituary I
thumbed and paused, a feeling tight as a cord knotted and tied
around my bicep.

~

I can see his girl strum her fingers through his hair, as in the
distance giant tankers hunkered along the horizon line for the
long haul to the open sea.

She is a while saying nothing. She feels selfish, an ache that
pushes through the chest. This is nothing more than sad.

They never fought. It should have been enough to live.

~

And then she saw it rising: the great blue heron, flying right
above their heads, over the edge of the shore, like an omen, of
the end of anything we've been toughened by—

~

A sort of salvation shuddered—

when all the world we mourn returns inside you—

like the wind through a shawl of enormous summer trees—

LISA ALLEN

Notes for My Daughter As She Preps for Her Most Public Sexual Assault[1]

Carefully choose a plausible aggressor, even better if he's had a brush or two with law enforcement. Avoid frat boys, legacy boys, football gods, swim team stars. Daddy's buddies and money and all. Be sure to put your best foot forward: pick the right clothes[2], the perfect color lipstick[3]. Remember to smile.

Choose your company for the night wisely: three is a good number, but only if all three will testify so it's best to plan for backups. You never know who might fall ill, who might refuse to remember, who might need to repay a debt. Make sure at least one has the stomach to watch it all go down—talk to this friend first, assure her she's being your best friend when she doesn't turn away, when she memorizes the curling corner of your attacker's lip, notices the brand name of his shoes. Make watching easy for this friend; for this to happen, you have to lead your rapist to an open space, a place easily accessed by others. Steer clear of basements, abandoned buildings, his backseat in a quiet park. Make sure you ask a different friend for a ride home. Work on your talking points now: if this friend doesn't mention your torn clothing, your smeared lipstick, find a way to casually bring it up in conversation. Remember to take a selfie with this friend—don't forget to smile.

---

1 I want nothing more than for you to never need this. Statistics say you will, that I did, that two of the three friends you met at freshman orientation already have. When this time comes you'll be forced to learn a new language. You'll learn to scan bloated briefs for hidden clues, to read between the lines.

2 Nothing too short, too tight, too sheer, too skimpy, too pretty, too complementary, too revealing, too kinky*, too interesting, too provocative, too feminine, too, too, too. *Nothing that might stoke a clichéd fantasy: librarian, cheerleader, teacher, nurse, secretary, nun. Yes, nun.

3 This is important: it's not about the best color to complement your skin; it's about the best color that shows up on photos. No nudes, no beige, no flesh-tone lipsticks. No. You need MAC Lady Danger or Dior 999. No glosses; they rub off too easily. You need a good, old-fashioned, matte stain. You need it to leave a mark.

Better yet, video the ride[4]. Geo tag it. Back it up to the cloud.

Practice giving your testimony. Stand before the mirror, repeat every detail until you can do so dry eyed. Watch your mannerisms: do you tuck your hair behind your ear? Maintain eye contact too long? Shift from side to side? Stop it. Practice saying I'm sorry and of course and yes, sir. Remember this isn't an admission of wrongdoing. It's expected so please understand: if you fail to recount the event just right, the jury of your peer's attackers will dismiss you without hearing another word you say.

Do you remember what it means to be conciliatory[5]? Choose your wardrobe for the inquisition: tasteful, professional, but not marmish; you want to strike that delicate balance between Jackie and Marilyn, Hepburn and Bardot. Solid colors look best on camera. Keep your hair on the long side but be sure it's shiny and neat; the men asking the questions tend to prefer it that way. A little makeup but not too much[6]. Glasses might help you look smarter. Wear a watch—don't ask me why, but I read somewhere that leaders and people of worth wear watches. Think back to when we played dress-up and sat at your tiny table for cups of invisible tea: remember how we practiced perfect posture, posed our pinkies in the most lady-like way? This is dress-up too, a grown-up kind of pretend.

After the assault: carefully undress and package your clothing in gallon-sized Ziploc bags. Swab under your nails, inside your mouth, wherever your rapist penetrated you. Save the cotton

---

4 You'll need enough storage on your phone to capture video, so I've prepaid for unlimited cloud storage in perpetuity. The good folks at Apple offer a mother/daughter plan.

5 Conciliatory (adj): intended or likely to placate or pacify. Appeasing. Pleasing. Say yes ma'am and no sir, please and thank you. Avert your eyes so as not to appear aggressive. Use your sweetest, quietest voice. Nuance here matters, so I need you to practice: it's acceptable for your voice to crack, for you to seem as if you're about to cry but not to show too much emotion, to cry too much, to break down. See: histrionics, hysterical, unreliable witness.

6 This would be a good time to wear the nude, the beige, the flesh-tone gloss. Clinique Long Last Glosswear in Tender Heart or Bobbi Brown High Shimmer Lip Gloss in Bare Sparkle are nice.

swabs, mark each by body part. Label everything appropriately
and store it all in our safety deposit box.[7]

Now it's time to make your phone calls: representative's office,
press 2 to report details of your most recent attack; doctor's office,
press 3 to leave a message; police department, press 1 to be direct-
ed to the automated assault clearing line; each friend with you the
night of the attack, to remind them they witnessed your undoing.
Take notes in your calendar, including the time of each call.[8]

A note about calling your representative's office: lines start to jam
mid-day so make yourself a cup of tea and dial before it's cool
enough to chug. Have regional office numbers ready; you might
have to call multiple lines before you find someone willing to help.
When a staffer answers, ignore the routine of it all, the robotic
tone with which your report is accepted. But don't be fooled. Be
ready for the hoops, for hold time. They want to see if you can
hack it, if you have what it takes to persist. You do. Steep more
tea. Stand at your open window and watch a squirrel scramble
along your deck rail, flatten itself when it notices you. Watch
leaves change from green to grunge to rust, but don't relent to
the romantic notion of a gorgeous Fall; instead stand witness to
the dying of it all. You're strong enough to see the difference.

Keep your checklist handy. It's your job to make sure the staffer
records your assaulter's name and social security number, the
exact time and coordinates of the assault, and names of your
corroborating witnesses. Once you've heard this staffer read the
information back to you, ask for a confirmation number. Write
it in your calendar in the square marked today. Store that calen-
dar in a Ziploc bag, in our family box (there are extra checklists
there; grab one before you go so you're ready for the next time).

---

7 I've included your name on our family box; when you visit, you'll see my
calendars and those that belong to your grandmother, your aunt, my best
friend from 2nd grade. It's our shared time capsule, an addendum to your
baby book, your yearbooks, your stacks of posed photos and saved greeting
cards.

8 It seems a bit too much, I realize, but even our First Lady says women need
"really hard evidence" to even suggest an assault occurred.

Call me. Anytime. Day, night, drunk, sober, happy, sad, worried, mad. Once, twice, thirty-seven times. Just call.

Remember: this list of instructions applies only to planned attacks. There will be others—many will be micro and seemingly meaningless: a man might cup your buttocks at a crowded concert and feign ignorance when you make eye contact; another might follow you down the street, leer, offer assessments of your body; yet another might pose as your boss, your teacher, your preacher, a relative and whisper in your ear, suggest you never tell. Some will cut emotional scars; others will leave bruises. All will hurt. I have no instructions for these save my own stories and the stories of women I love. Is this my greatest failing, as your mother, how I send you into the world with a shield so easily ripped apart?

One final note: treat yourself kindly. Work time into your daily schedule to reflect. Bullet-point details of your day, every day, in your calendar. I read once about a husband who, before he died, arranged for a flower delivery to his wife on every subsequent birthday. He left dozens of notes with his florist, dates of future deliveries penned in curly-cue cursive on heavy, cream envelopes. The idea of flowers makes me smile, but only until I remember that flowers, too, die and it's up to us (the mothers, the daughters) to throw them away, mop up the mess. I can't bear the thought of burdening you with that, sweet soul; I can't send you a monthly reminder of shriveling. Of rot. Not when it's already in and around us, not when we are expected to swallow it all. Instead of flowers I've arranged a delivery of pens, a new bunch every birthday. Forgive me for spoiling the surprise but I can't wait for whatever comes next; I'm too happy remembering how your face lit up on your eighth birthday when you unwrapped a Costco-size box of gel pens: rainbow rows of every color that you used for homework, for sketching, for endearing notes you left on my pillow on random afternoons, your penmanship awkward and loopy and tirelessly joyful. My one wish: don't save these pens for a special day. Use every pen so often the ink runs dry: grassy green for grocery lists, ocean-water blue to send cards to your brothers, tattoo black to write poetry, essays, letters to your

elected officials. On assault days, use one of the red pens—not
the red of Valentine's Day hearts or summer watermelon slurp.
Write the details you know others will want to hear in cherry
juice red, blotchy and real.

ROZ KUBEK

Before the Call Comes

October's seals
river grass

a cell tower
gray sky

osprey in air
a boat unmoored

I know
you're somewhere
breathing.

QUINTIN COLLINS

At Night, I Tuck a Pillow Beneath My Arm to Sleep

Half-empty High Life in hand, Jack Daniels shot on the bar,
my old plush kangaroo looks like he has had a long day.

Dollar sign tattoo on his chest, a marker memento
I scrawled when I was five years old, he sips beer.

It weeps from a wound in his arm. My mother
never had the hole stitched at the stuffed animal hospital.

He still has both eyes and a sutured leg. I do not
ask where he has been. I question only his choice of beer.

He cocks his head but says nothing, just takes the shot,
then swallows his last gulps of lager, frayed stuffing

soaked and stained. Hobbling off the barstool, he pays
with quarters I stashed in his pouch decades ago.

He tips with pennies I dug out of couches.
He leaves. I follow him outside, where he beckons

for me to come home with him. I am drunk,
it is late, and I have work in the morning.

He limps away, dragging his busted leg
like a boulder. I stumble home, tumble into bed.

QUINTIN COLLINS

The Dandelion Speaks of Survival

Written for the Pine Manor College graduating class of 2018.

When they see me rise, a nebula of coronas, sun-
bursting spires strewn among their bermuda and bluegrass lawns,
they will come for me. When my roots fan a maze
around their chrysanthemums, interlace a cage
around their petunias, grab the life I'm so often denied,
they will come for me. They will come for me
when I yawn from a driveway fissure. They will come for me
when my jagged leaves sprawl over their gravel beds.
They will come with hands clenched, garden shears
snapping jaws, weed wackers to split my body,
chemicals that wither and disintegrate me. They will come
with mower blades sharp, the thunder of gasoline
combusting in the engine. They will come
with tillers and hoes and rakes and knives and torches.
Don't they know that when the wind rocks my halo,
I cast seeds into the wind? Don't they know
I clutch earth tighter than any English bluebell? Don't they know
I have survived their hands and their instruments. Don't they know
I have survived every way they have spilled my bitter milk.
I survive. I survive. I survive.
I will survive again and again. When they sharpen their new tools,
when they arm themselves with professional-grade sprays,
when they call their landscapers to scrape out my existence,
when they call me weed, when they call me nuisance,
when they call me pest, when they say I am not welcome,
when they poison their own soil to stunt my growth,
know that I will survive. Know that I will spring forth
a field of gold, glisten with my petals kissed by morning dew.
Know that I will bloom like the sun spilling
over the horizon. Know that I will stretch my stem and roots
beyond all borders. I will split their concrete and this earth.

MICHAEL MERCURIO

The Unbnd Verses by Kwame Opoku-Duku
(Glass Poetry Press 2018, $8.50)

Kwame Opoku-Duku and I follow each other on Twitter, and have interacted on that platform several times, always in positive ways. I've enjoyed the individual poems he has shared there, as well as his interviews with other poets (such as Devin Gael Kelly). So, I was excited to read his chapbook *The Unbnd Verses* (2018, Glass Poetry Press) because I sensed a keen and thoughtful poet at work.

And so I had. *The Unbnd Verses* unfolds more with each reading, as I learn to read Opoku-Duku's personal poetics, to follow his leaps and turns through poems that shimmer with holy music:

> the rain has ended, and up the block Lauryn Hill blasts
>
> out of the back of somebody's car.

> And they pray that I violate.
>
> They pray to you, Lord.

> I've been murdered by the eyes
>
> of thousands. (i. *Ghosts*, p.1)

In these lines I hear the percussive sounds of consonants — the /d/ and /b/ sounds, the /k/ of "block" and "car", and the gradual giving way to the vowels found in "eyes" and "thousands". I also hear echoes of Paul Celan, particularly his poem "Tenebrae", with its invocation "Pray to us, Lord./We are near." and its amplification of the voices of the silenced dead. The poems in this chapbook also amplify voices, though not of Celan's silenced dead, but rather those living lives made difficult — sometimes deadly — by racism. I have wrestled with how to quote or excerpt these poems, given the essential and nuanced manner in which Opuko-Duku uses variations of the n-word as integral elements in his poems. In reading these poems I never felt unwelcome, or like I was being shown something I should never see, but I was certainly aware that these are poems that make use of language and poetics that my own writing will never access.

And this is no bad thing. In fact, it is a good thing to read poems that are challenging (and also, in this case, beautiful and lyrical) and to wrestle with how one responds to them. I like to say, half-joking, that poetry is the closest thing to telepathy that we humans will ever experience, but the serious side of that is that we can briefly enter the world of the poet through their words and voice. And so I will never know the same sense or the same experience as Kwame, but I am no longer able to consider just my own sense or experience, either. So I am changed, and the speaker of the poems changes, too:

> i see you my son i'm looking at you i can see that
> the lord wants to work through you the lord favors
> you he wants you to own your own business the lord
> has a woman picked out for you son the lord's will
> the lord willing my son guide you through the lord son
> has a plan the lord wants my son he wants my son in
> mysterious ways my son the lord wants you to go to Africa
> the lord is the lord is the one who can guide you through
> this time son the lord lives the lord lifts up your troubles
> son he wants the lord to heal you son i'm looking at you
> son i see you son i've got chills all over lord my body lord
> the lord my son my body what is it that you want my son
> *have you ever truly wondered what it is you have*
> (viii. prophe-see, p.17)

What are we to make of this burst of familiar phrases, of stock exhortations like "the lord favors/you" and "the lord lifts up your troubles", of the familiar-yet-distant "son", of the lower-case "i" throughout? The speaker in this poem feels to me like an elder (or "old head", as other poems throughout the collection might have it) trying to reach across a generational divide through the rhetoric and rhythm of religious invocation. I hear the voice of a humbled messenger of divine truth, but I also hear the voice of a parent who cares clumsily, without a nuanced understanding of this son who may not want to hear all of these things the lord wants him to do. It's a vulnerable, desperate speaker I hear, rushing to connect, pinned between the lord and the son. The tension in this poem, pulled taut by the lack of punctuation, is never resolved. We don't know if the son hears the parent's exhortations. We don't know anything after the last line ejects us from the poem: "*have you ever truly wondered what it is you have*".

Opoku-Duku's precise use of tone in these poems is a marvel, and showcased so well in "ix. afro-beat paradise with the disembodied spirit who now believes he can love":

> i'm sho there was
> times I talked slick in
> the past
>
> &
>
> everything i'm about
> to say is true
>
> (beat)
>
> i want to take you back
> to africa/ i want to father
> many children with you/
> dress them with red earth
> & leaves/ put their photos
> on instagram for all the
> haters to behold (p.18)

The full poem, which runs another 8 stanzas, maintains this heightened tone, which rings of the promises made by one person to another in an attempt at seduction, and we the readers are led to wonder how sincere these words are. Is this a speaker who believes these words himself, or is this a speaker who is manipulating us? Is the speaker working to convince himself of the existence of an afro-beat paradise, beyond the effect of "all the haters" and in the rarified realm of Michelin-starred restaurants? The first ampersand feels like a leaning-in, the creation of a physical intimacy (desired or not — that, I think, is up to the reader.)

There are three intrusions on this narrative; the first takes the form of parenthetical stage direction-like notation to indicate that the speaker has paused, which you can see in the excerpt quoted above. The second is similar, though more complex: "(short beat, *thinks of words carefully*)". We're given a view of the speaker's thought process here, at a time when the intensity of the discourse increases, with 4 short lines putting tremendous pressure on the words:

> to
> only
> dream
> in twi

Each line feels like someone leaning in, speaking low and forceful directly in the reader's ear to lodge this notion directly into the reader's mind. And then, after these four lines expend their power, there is the lean-back with another ampersand, followed by a stanza that leaps to a future in which the speaker and the reader have become a "we" who return to their children after a vacation together. This is where the third intrusion on the narrative exists, in the voice of the children singing:

> *mama & papa have come*
> *home to see their children/*
> *now the war is over*
>
> *mama & papa have come*
> *home to see their children/*
> *now we will have peace* (p. 19-20)

What I read as this poem's physical choreography is remarkable, giving the sense of motion, of intimacy, of setting without ever actually describing the here-and-now of the speaker and the addressee. And I'm reading this as a seduction in a bar or a club, but that's the baggage of my experience, and I suspect anyone who reads this with different experiences will understand that choreography in a different setting — but still as choreography.

Due to limitations of time and space I chose to focus on some exemplary poems from this chapbook, but I do want to call out the series of linked poems that occur throughout *The Unbnd Verses*, sharing the title "the old head verses (ecclesiastes)" followed by the numbered lines contained in each poem. The Biblical book of Ecclesiastes, traditionally attributed to Solomon, is one of the "Wisdom Books" of the Judeo-Christian tradition, and it engages with "the big questions", including the meaning of life. So, too, do "the old head verses", functioning as a collection of wisdom passed from elder speaker(s) to younger listeners, without judgment flowing from either side. This voice, or these voices, carry deep affection for a beloved-but-imperfect community, an identity that grows with each successive generation.

CONTRIBUTORS

CONTRIBUTORS

CLARISSA ADKINS' poems are published in *Poems2Go, Parentheses, The Pinch*, and more. She was a finalist for the 17th Annual Erskine J. Poetry Prize with *Smartish Pace*. For over a year, she has enjoyed being a reader for *Sugar House Review*. Clarissa earned her MFA in poetry from Lesley University in 2018, and she teaches yoga and high school English around Richmond, Virginia.

JONATHAN AIBEL has read in the Brookline Poetry Series, where he frequently contributes to their open mike. Jonathan has studied with Lucie Brock-Broido and Henri Cole. His poems have been published in *The Aurorean, Mason's Road* and *Round Magazine*. His work appears in the anthology *Rhyme and Punishment* from Local Gems Press.

JOSETTE AKRESH-GONZALES is a production editor at a medical publisher. Her work has been included in *PANK, Juxtaprose, Lime Hawk, Literary Orphans, Black Heart Magazine, The Good Men Project, Knee-Jerk*, and *Matter*, among others. Also, *Black Heart Magazine* chose her poem "Happy New Year" for their Best of 2014 issue, and *PANK* ran an interview with her on their blog. While a student at Boston University (1997–2001), she co-founded the BU Literary Society and the journal *Clarion* and was its editor for two years. You can find her on Twitter @Vivakresh.

LISA ALLEN'S work has appeared in *Listen to Your Mother: What She Said Then, What We're Saying Now* (Putnam 2015), *Bacopa Literary Review* (2018), and *Feckless Cunt* (2018). Lisa holds an MFA in Creative Nonfiction from The Solstice Low-Residency MFA in Creative Writing Program at Pine Manor College, where she was a Michael Steinberg Fellow in Creative Nonfiction. She is pursuing an MFA in Poetry, also at Solstice.

ANTHONY G AMSTERDAM is a lawyer specializing in death-penalty defense and civil rights litigation. His poetry reflects this landscape.

ALEXIS AVLAMIS (b. Athens 1979) is a painter influenced by the Surrealist's Automatism. He is a laureate of the International Emerging Artist Award, the 2018 American Art Awards (Naive category,) and the Art Slant showcase prize (Painting). He has exhibited internationally, and many private and museum collections display his works.

KAY BELL is a bibliophile who can be quoted, "If it makes me cry, sweat or bleed, then it is worth writing about." She has been published in *Brown Molasses Sunday: An Anthology of Black Women Writers* and online by *Moko: Caribbean Arts and Letters, The Write Launch*, and *PRONG & PROSY*. She is an MFA candidate at The City College of New York.

SHEILA BLACK is the author of four poetry collections, most recently *Iron, Ardent* (Educe Press 2017.) Her poems have appeared in *Poetry, Puerto del Sol,*

Willow Springs, the *Birmingham Review* and elsewhere. She currently divides her time between Washington, DC and San Antonio, Texas.

BRENDA BLIGHT is an artist whose emotionally resonant and beautiful works challenge assertions.

ACE BOGGESS is the author of four books of poetry, most recently *I Have Lost the Art of Dreaming It So* (Unsolicited Press, 2018) and *Ultra Deep Field* (Brick Road Poetry Press, 2017,) and the novel, *A Song Without a Melody* (Hyperborea Publishing, 2016). His writing has appeared in *Harvard Review*, *Mid-American Review*, *RATTLE*, *River Styx*, *North Dakota Quarterly* and many other journals. He lives in Charleston, West Virginia.

LAURE-ANNE BOSSELAAR is the author of *The Hour Between Dog and*

Wolf, *Small Gods of Grief*, winner of the Isabella Gardner Prize for Poetry, and *A New Hunger*, selected as a Notable Book by the American Library Association. Sungold Editions published her chapbook *Rooms Remembered*. Her latest collection *These Many Rooms* was published by Four Way Books. With her husband Kurt Brown, she translated a book by Flemish poet, *Herman de Coninck: The Plural of Happiness*. The recipient of a Pushcart Prize, and the editor of four poetry anthologies, she taught at Emerson College, Sarah Lawrence College, UCSB; and, she is a member of the core faculty at the Low Residency MFA in Creative Writing Program of Pine Manor College in Boston.

M. A. BOWERSOCK's writing has appeared previously in *Crab Orchard Review*, *Boston Review*, and *Michigan Quarterly Review*, among other publications. Bowersock is a graduate of the MFA program at the University of Michigan and currently lives in eastern Idaho.

MICHELLE BROOKS has published a collection of poetry, *Make Yourself*

Small, (Backwaters Press), and a novella, *Dead Girl, Live Boy*, (Storylandia Press). Her poetry collection, *Flamethrower*, will be published by Latte Press in 2019. A native Texan, she has spent much of her adult life in Detroit.

ROBERT CARR is the author of *Amaranth*, a chapbook published in 2016 by Indolent Books, and a 2017 Pushcart Prize-nominated poet. His poetry has appeared in the *Bellevue Literary Review*, *Radius Literary Magazine*, and other publications. His work is forthcoming in *Crab Orchard Review*, *Rattle*, and *The Massachusetts Review*. Robert's first full-length collection of poetry, *The Unbuttoned Eye*, will be released in 2019 by 3: A Taos Press. He serves as an associate poetry editor for Indolent Books and is also Deputy Director for the Bureau of Infectious Disease and Laboratory Sciences in Massachusetts. Follow Carr at robertcarr.org.

RUTH CHAD is a psychologist who lives and works in the Boston area. Her poems have appeared in the *Aurorean*, *Bagels with the Bards*, *Connection Psychoanalytic: Couple and Family Institute of New England*, *Constellations*, *Ibbetson Street*, *Montreal Poems* and elsewhere. Her chapbook, *The Sound of Angels*, was published by

Cervena Barva Press in 2017.

QUINTIN COLLINS is a poet, managing editor, and Solstice MFA program graduate from the Chicago area, who currently lives in Boston. His works have appeared or are forthcoming in *Threshold magazine, Glass Mountain, Eclectica Magazine, Transition Magazine* and elsewhere.

SUSAN EYRE COPPOCK is a writer from Massachusetts. She published *Cardinal Days: A Coming-of-Age Memoir* in 2016.

LORI CORRY is a year-round resident of Nantucket Island, MA. She spends her time investigating and gaining creative inspiration from the stories and myths of the world's goddesses and her teenage son. She works at a small independent school where she's a business manager and a mindfulness teacher.

JENIFER DEBELLIS' debut poetry collection, *Blood Sisters*, is now available from Main Street Rag (2018). She's *Pink Panther Magazine*'s executive editor and directs the Detroit Writers' Guild. She earned her MFA in Creative Writing from Solstice of Pine Manor College. A former writer-in-residence for the Meadow Brook Writing Project, she facilitates workshops for Oakland University's MBWP Writing Camps. JDB teaches writing and literature for Saginaw Valley State University and Macomb Community College. Nominated for a 2018 Pushcart Prize, her work appears in AWP's *Festival Writer*, the *Good Men Project, Literary Orphans, Sliver of Stone, Solstice Literary Magazine* and other excellent journals. Find her at JeniferDeBellis.com.

SEAN THOMAS DOUGHERTY is the author or editor of 16 books including *The Second O of Sorrow* (2018 BOA Editions). He lives in Erie, PA where he works as a Med Tech and caregiver for people recovering from traumatic brain injuries. His website is seanthomasdoughertypoet.com.

JAY FEATHERSTONE has had careers as an editor and literary critic for the *New Republic*, a peace activist against the Vietnam War, a lecturer at Harvard, the headmaster of the Commonwealth School in Boston, faculty leader of a school-based teacher education program at Michigan State University, and, as a poet, author of *Brace's Cove* (New Issues, 2000), and *Glass* (Fenway Press, 2019).

FEDERICO FEDERICI (1974) is a physicist and prize-winning writer whose works have appeared in several print and online publications including *3:AM Magazine* and *Raum*. His books, include *"L'opera racchiusa"* (2009, Lorenzo Montano Prize), *"Appunti dal passo del lupo"* (2013) in the book series curated by Eugenio De Signoribus, *"Dunkelwort"* (2015), *"Mrogn"* (2017, Elio Pagliarani Prize) He has been awarded the Lorenzo Montano Prize for prose. Detailed information available on his website: http://federicofederici.net

ROBBIE GAMBLE holds an MFA in poetry from Lesley University. His poems have appeared in *Scoundrel Time, Writers Resist, Stonecoast Review, Solstice*, and *Poet Lore*. He was the winner of the 2017 Carve Poetry prize. He works as a nurse practitioner caring for homeless people in Boston, Massachusetts.

CLAUDIA GARY is the author of *Humor Me* (David Robert Books, 2006) and several chapbooks including *Bikini Buyer's Remorse*. Her poems appear in anthologies including *Villanelles* (Everyman Press, 2012), *Forgetting Home* (Barefoot Muse Press, 2013), and *The Great American Wise Ass Poetry Anthology* (Lamar University, 2015), as well as in journals internationally. A three-time finalist for the Howard Nemerov Sonnet Award, she has chaired various panels at the West Chester University (Pa.) Poetry Conference and the Frost Farm Poetry Conference. Currently, she gives Sonnet, Villanelle, and Meter workshops at The Writer's Center (writer.org). She also sings, composes art songs and tonal chamber music, and writes articles on health for The *VVA Veteran* and other magazines. For more information: pw.org/content/claudia_gary. Follow her at @claudiagary

JOEY GOULD, a writing tutor at Framingham State University, is a longtime contributor to Mass Poetry as a poet, workshop leader, event coordinator, and content writer. They lead generative poetry workshops at Student Day of Poetry events across Massachusetts. They have performed in improv poetry events, two poetry circuses and The Poetry Society of New York's Poetry Brothel. While they work to make space for others as lead poetry editor for *Drunk Monkeys*, their poems have appeared in *Five:2: One, The Compassion Anthology, District Lit*, and *Memoir Mixtapes*.

SEKYO NAM HAINES, born and raised in South Korea, immigrated to the U.S. in 1973 as a registered nurse. She studied American literature and writing at the Goddard College ADP, and poetry with the late Ottone M. Riccio in Boston, MA. Her poems have appeared in the anthologies, *Do Not Give Me Things Unbroken, Unlocking the Poem*, and *Beyond Words*, and in the poetry journal *Off the Coast*. Her translations of Korean poetry have appeared in *Notre Dame Review, The Massachusetts Review, The Harvard Review* and elsewhere. Sekyo lives in Cambridge, MA with her family.

GREY HELD is a recipient of a National Endowment for the Arts Fellowship in Creative Writing. His books include *Two-Star General* (by Brick Road PoetryPress in 2012), *Spilled Milk* (by Word Press in 2013), and *WORKaDAY* (byFutureCycle Press in 2019.) He works closely with the Mayor's Office of CulturalAffairs in Newton, MA to direct projects that connect contemporary poets (and their poetry) with a broader audience.

BARBARA HELFGOTT HYETT is a poet, teacher, and scholar who has published five collections of poetry. The most recent is *Rift* (Univ. of Arkansas Press). Her poems have appeared in small literary and major national magazines in America, and abroad. She has won the Boston Foundation's Artist Fellowship Award, two Massachusetts Cultural Council Fellowships, the Sproat Award for teaching English at Boston University. She has also taught writing and literature at MIT, Harvard, and Holy Cross. She directs PoemWorks: The Workshop for Publishing Poets, in Newton, MA (http//www.poemworks.com).

CAROL HOBBS is originally from Newfoundland, Canada. She lives, writes poetry and teaches high school English in Massachusetts. Her poems have appeared in *The Malahat Review, Fiddlehead, The Antigonish Review, Cider Press Review, Appalachian Heritage, Riddle Fence* and other journals and anthologies in Canada, Ireland, and the United States.

MARY ANN HONAKER is the author of *It Will Happen Like This* (YesNo Press, 2015). Her poems have appeared in *2 Bridges, The Dudley Review, Euphony, Juked, Off the Coast, Van Gogh's Ear, The Lake* and elsewhere. Mary Ann holds a BA in philosophy from West Virginia University, a master of theological studies degree from Harvard Divinity School, and an MFA in creative writing from Lesley University. She currently lives in Beckley, West Virginia.

CINDY HOUSE earned her MFA from Lesley University in 2017 and won an emerging artist grant from the St. Botolph Club Foundation in 2018. Her work has been published in *The Rumpus, The Drum, So to Speak, Wigleaf, Longleaf Review,* and *Driftwood Press*. She opened for David Sedaris several times last year, and is scheduled to open in more cities in 2019. She lives in New Haven, CT with her husband and son.

HEATHER HUGHES is a poet, a letterpress printer, and Associate Editor at Harvard University Press. Her work appears in journals such as *The Adroit Journal, Boxcar Poetry Review, decomP, Denver Quarterly, Gulf Coast, Painted Bride Quarterly, The Rumpus,* and *Sidereal Magazine*. She can be found online at birdmaddgirl.com.

MANI G. IYER is a deaf-blind poet, born and raised in Bombay, India and now residing in Massachusetts. His poems have appeared in *Off the Coast, Poems2Go* and *The Helicon Poetry Journal* (translated to Hebrew.) His chapbook, *Water Festival,* was selected as a finalist in the 2017 Letterpress chapbook competition.

KONNER JEBB is a recent poetry graduate from the Solstice MFA Program of Pine Manor College. He is currently published in *Strange Horizons, Trans Cafe,* and *Poems2Go*.

CHRISTINE JONES is a massage/physical therapist and an MFA graduate from Lesley University. She's founder/chief-editor of *poems2go,* a public poetry project. Her poetry is published at *32 poems, Salamander, Crab Creek Review, Naugatuck River Review, Cimarron Review* and elsewhere. She often swims or surfs alongside her husband, near their home in Cape Cod, MA.

HAYUN KIM is a homeschooled senior living in South Korea. She is working on her portfolio in preparation for university. Her other hobbies are fashion design, reading, and going to the movies.

ROSELYN KUBEK has had her poetry published in several journals, including the *Stonecoast Review, The Weekly Avocet, NCTE's English Journal, Leaflet,* and *Pink Panther Magazine.*

MATEO LARA is from Bakersfield, California. He received his B.A. in English at CSU Bakersfield and is currently working on his M.F.A. in Poetry at Randolph College in Lynchburg, VA. His poems have been featured in *Orpheus*, *EOAGH*, *Empty Mirror*, and *The New Engagement*. He is an editor for *RabidOak* online literary journal & Zoetic Press.

SARAH KIRSTINE LAIN is the Managing Editor of *Poems2go*, and her work has appeared in *B O D Y*, *Rivista Letteraria*, *Salt Creek Journal*, and *Lily Poetry Review*. She is the Assistant Director of Research Innovation for the University of Chicago's Office of Research and National Labs and earned an MFA in poetry from Lesley University. Lain has worked in defense simulation training development, taught writing courses for the Art Institute of Tampa, and has hosted many art collaborations for human rights. Her interests include how STEM interconnects with poetry in the context of emotionally-restricted cultures.

JON D. LEE is the author of three books, including *An Epidemic of Rumors: How Stories Shape Our Perceptions of Disease* and *These Around Us*. His poems and essays have appeared or are forthcoming in *Sierra Nevada Review*, *The Writer's Chronicle*, *Connecticut River Review*, *The Laurel Review*, *Inflectionist Review*, and *Oregon Literary Review*. He earned an MFA in Poetry from Lesley University and a Ph.D. in Folklore. Lee teaches at Suffolk University and spends his spare time with his wife and children.

EVE LINN received her B.A. cum laude from Smith College in Fine Art and her M.F.A. in Poetry from Lesley University. She has attended the Bread Loaf Writer's Conference, the Frost Place Conference on Poetry and the Colrain Manuscript Conference. She is a published poet and book reviewer. Her favorite color is blue. She collects antique baby shoes, vintage textiles and pottery. She lives west of Boston with her family, and two cats.

FRANCIS LUNNEY's poems have been published by *The Owen Wister Review*, *Outside Bozeman*, *Appalachia*, and *Salamander*. He also had a poem featured on WCAI (Cape Cod's NPR station) radio's *Poetry Sunday* program.

MARY LOU MALONEY is a poet and former lobbyist for the Arc of Massachusetts, an organization that represents developmentally delayed people. She has studied poetry under Barbara Helfgott Hyett and is a member of Poemworks: The Workshop for Publishing Poets. She received her undergraduate degree from Regis College and her Masters from Boston College.

JENNIFER MARTELLI is the author of *My Tarantella* (Bordighera Press), as well as the chapbook, *After Bird* (Grey Book Press, 2017). Her work has appeared or will appear in *The Sycamore Review*, *Sugar House*, *Superstition Review*, *Thrush* and *Tinderbox Poetry Journal*. Her prose and artwork have been published in *Five-2-One*, *The Baltimore Review* and *Green Mountains Review*. Jennifer Martelli has been nominated for Pushcart and Best of the Net Prizes and is the recipient of the Massachusetts Cultural Council Grant in Poetry. She is a poetry editor for *The Mom Egg Review*.

MARTHA MCCOLLOUGH is a writer and video artist living in Chelsea, Massachusetts. She has an MFA in painting from Pratt Institute. Her poems have appeared or are forthcoming in the *Tampa Review*, *The Baffler*, *Cream City Review*, *Crab Creek Review* and *Salamander*, among others. Her videopoems have appeared in *Triquarterly*, *Datableed* and *Atticus Review*.

MICHAEL MERCURIO lives and writes in the Pioneer Valley of Massachusetts. His work has appeared in the *Indianapolis Review* and *Crab Creek Review*. You can find him at poetmercurio.com

SUZANNE MERCURY is a poet who creates mixed-media visual and haptic poetry assemblages using found objects, old book pages, LED lights, glass, gold, tree branches, and all manner of natural materials to go with her written work. She has published poetry in a variety of literary journals including *SpoKe*, *Truck*, *Summer Stock*, *Sonora Review*, and *Hayden's Ferry Review*, as well as in anthologies *Let the Bucket Down* and *The Wisdoms of the Universes in a Single String of Letters*.

MARY MERIAM co-founded Headmistress Press. She edits *Lavender Review* (lesbian poetry and art). Poems from her new collection, *My Girl's Green Jacket*, have appeared in *Prelude*, *Cimarron Review*, *Crab Orchard Review*, *The Awl*, *The Gay & Lesbian Review*, *Adrienne*, *Rattle* and *Women's Review of Books*. A new poem appeared recently in *Poetry*.

DAVID P. MILLER's chapbook, *The Afterimages*, was published by Červená Barva Press. His poems have recently appeared in *Meat for Tea*, *riverbabble*, *Nixes Mate Review*, *Naugatuck River Review*, and *HedgeApple*, among others. His poem "Kneeling Woman and Dog," first published in *Meat for Tea*, was included in the 2015 edition of *Best Indie Lit New England*. With a background in experimental theater before turning to poetry, David was a member of the multidisciplinary Mobius Artists Group of Boston for 25 years. He was a librarian at Curry College in Milton, Mass., from which he retired in June 2018.

CHELL NAVARRO holds an MFA in Poetry from the University of Missouri-Kansas City. To afford her lavish lifestyle as a poet, she works as a waitress, and for a literary nonprofit. She lives in Kansas City, but her spiritual home is Taos, New Mexico. The poem published is part of a larger project of ekphrastic poems, based on the early drawings of Georgia O'Keeffe.

KATHY NILSSON earned a BA in English Literature from Mount Holyoke College and an MFA in poetry from the Bennington Writing Seminars. She has received fellowships from the MacDowell Colony and The New York State Writer's Institute. Her poems have appeared in *Ploughshares*, *Boston Review*, *Poetry Daily*, *Columbia*, *Volt*, and other literary journals. Her chapbook, *The Abattoir*, was published by Finishing Line Press in 2008. She is a recipient of the Poetry Society of America's Robert H. Winner Award. Her full-length poetry collection, *The Infant Scholar* (2015) is published by Tupelo Press. She lives in Cambridge, MA., with her husband and son.

REBECCA HART OLANDER's poetry has appeared recently in *Ilanot Review*, *Plath Poetry Project*, *Solstice*, and others. Collaborative work, made with Elizabeth Paul, has been published in *They Said: A Multi-Genre Anthology of Contemporary Collaborative Writing* (BLP) and online at *Duende*. Rebecca won the 2013 Women's National Book Association poetry contest and has been nominated for a Pushcart Prize. She lives in Western Massachusetts, where she teaches writing at Westfield State University. She is the editor/director of Perugia Press. Find her at rebeccahartolander.com.

MIRIAM O'NEAL's poems and reviews have appeared in *Blackbird Journal*, *Nottingham Review*, *Ragazine*, *Solidago Journal* and in many other journals. Her book of poems, *We Start with What We're Given*, was published by Kelsay Books in July 2018. She also translates Italian poetry and has won various awards for her poems and translation of Alda Merini's *The Poem of the Cross*. She lives in Plymouth, MA.

STEVEN OSTROWSKI is a poet, fiction writer, painter, and songwriter. His work, including his artwork, appears widely in literary journals, magazines, and anthologies. He is the author of five published chapbooks. One of the chapbooks, *Seen/unseen*, is a collaboration written with his son Ben Ostrowski. He and Ben are also the authors of a full-length collection, *Penultimate Human Constellation*, published in 2018 by Tolsun Books. His chapbook, *After the Tate Modern*, won the Atlantic Road Prize and is published by Island Verse Editions. He teaches at Central Connecticut State University.

MICHAEL PETERS is a poet, visual poet, fictioneer, writer and musician. As the author of *Vaast Bin* (Calamari), and other assorted language art works, Peters uses sound-imaging tactics in both old and new media wherever environmental demands necessitate constrained indeterminacy, point-blank guessing, and ethical illumination. See also http://www.michael-peters.com/.

NAOMIE JEAN-PIERRE'S pen bleeds with the places she has been. She is an MA literature candidate at City College of New York, now finalizing her joint masters at the University of Paris 7. She hails from Haiti by way of Atlanta. She is a student/explorer by day and a literary chemist by night. Her works have been published in *Fiction Magazine*, *Noble Gas Qtrly*, *Mud Season Review*, *Rigorous Magazine* and more. She has recently been nominated for a Pushcart Prize.

KYLE POTVIN's chapbook, *Sound Travels on Water* (Finishing Line Press), won the 2014 Jean Pedrick Chapbook Award. She is a two-time finalist for the Howard Nemerov Sonnet Award. Her poems have appeared in *Bellevue Literary Review*, *Crab Creek Review*, *The New York Times*, *The Huffington Post*, *Measure*, *JAMA* and others. A member of the Powow River Poets and Hyla Brook Poets, she is an advisor to Frost Farm Poetry in Derry, NH, and helps produce the New Hampshire Poetry Festival.

RENUKA RAGHAVAN'S previous work has appeared in, *Boston Literary Magazine*, *Jersey Devil Press*, *Blink-Ink*, *Star 82 Review*, *Down in the Dirt Literary*

Magazine, *Chicago Literati*, and *Gravel*, among others. She is the author of *Out of the Blue* (Big Table Publishing, 2017), a collection of poetry and prose. She is a co-founder of the Poetry Sisters Collective and serves as the fiction book reviewer at Cervena Barva Press. She writes and lives in Massachusetts, with her family and beloved beagle. Visit her at www.renukaraghavan.com

ANDREA READ's poems have appeared most recently (or are forthcoming) in *Barrow Street*, *Black Rabbit Quarterly*, *Copper Nickel*, *FIELD*, *The Ilanot Review*, *Plume*, *The Missouri Review*, and *Tupelo Quarterly*. She is the recipient of a National Resource Fellowship, a Tinker Foundation Grant, and an Artist's Fellowship from the Somerville Arts Council. Andrea divides her time between Somerville, Massachusetts and Brooks, Maine, where she and her family tend 500 acres of forest.

STEVEN RIEL's first full-length book of poetry *Fellow Odd Fellow* was published by Trio House Press in 2013. He's also the author of three chapbooks, the most recent of which, *Postcard from P-town*, was runner-up for the inaugural Robin Becker Chapbook Prize and published by Seven Kitchens Press. His poems have appeared in several anthologies and numerous periodicals, including most recently *International Poetry Review* and *Naugatuck River Review*.

LISA RUA-WARE works as a technical writer in the software industry. She graduated from the University of Massachusetts in Amherst with a bachelor's degree in English Literature and earned a Master of Arts in English from Simmons College. Her poetry has appeared in the *San Pedro River Review* and *Muddy River Poetry Review*.

RIKKI SANTER's work has appeared in various publications including *Ms. Magazine*, *Poetry East*, *Margie*, *Hotel Amerika*, *The American Journal of Poetry*, *Slab*, *Crab Orchard Review*, *RHINO*, *Grimm*, *Slipstream*, *Midwest Review*, and *The Main Street Rag*. My fifth poetry collection, *Make Me That Happy* was recently awarded an Ohioana Book Award nomination.

MARIA SEBASTIAN is an American singer/songwriter and poet living in Clarence Center, NY. She writes mostly about the unsung among us□ those who press on against enormous odds, but remain mostly unnoticed. She also teaches public speaking and English in the SUNY system and plans to settle one day in Woodstock, NY. Visit www.mariasebastian.com or @paperspective

MATTHEW SISSON's poetry has appeared in magazines and journals such as *JAMA*, the *Journal of The American Medical Association* and the *Harvard Review Online*. He has been nominated for a Pushcart Prize, and his book *Please, Call Me Moby* was published by the Pecan Grove Press, St. Mary's University. He is the former poetry editor of *Modern Steel Construction* and has read his work on NPR's *On Point*.

SARAH J. SLOAT divides her time between Frankfurt and Barcelona, where she works in the news. Her poems, collage, and prose have appeared in *The Offing*, *Hayden's Ferry Review* and *Diagram*. She blogs at her website sarahjsloat.com.

DAVID SOMERSET lives in Salem, MA with his wife and small disagreeable dog. He writes and performs poetry, stories, and music at local open mikes and features. His work has been published in the *Merrimac Mic Anthology*, *Whisper and the Roar*, *Oddball magazine* and online. Dave also has published a chapbook, *Among Poets Tonight*.

FAYE SNIDER began to write poetry several decades ago while maintaining a full-time psychotherapy practice. She writes memoir and essays and earned an MFA in creative nonfiction at Pine Manor's MFA Solstice Program. Follow Snider's blog at fayewriter.com

DANIEL B. SUMMERHILL is a professor, poet and performance artist from Oakland, CA. A graduate of The Solstice Low Residency MFA program, his work has appeared or is forthcoming in *Califragile*, *Blavity*, *Button*, *Streetlight Press*, and others. His essay on black voice in writing is forthcoming from the Massachusetts Reading Association.

CLIMBING SUN is a world traveler, engineer, teacher, and poet. Born in Michigan, raised in Ohio, and educated in Florida, he designs structures in South Florida and California. He has taught poetry in elementary schools and spent 22 winters teaching a poetry writing workshop at the Montessori Junior High School in Santa Cruz, California. He currently resides in Boca Raton, Florida. His publications include *The Blue* (2013), his first novel, *Sundances* (2017), a prose-poem memoir, and *Parables & Myths* (2018), his first collection of verse poems. He holds a Bachelor of Civil Engineering degree from the University of Florida.

CAMMY THOMAS has published two collections of poems with Four Way Books: *Inscriptions* (2014), and *Cathedral of Wish*, which received the 2006 Norma Farber First Book Award from the Poetry Society of America. Her poems are forthcoming or have recently appeared in *Moon City Review*, *Nixes Mate*, *The Summerset Review*, *The Tampa Review*, and *The Missouri Review*. A fellowship from the Ragdale Foundation helped her complete *Inscriptions*. Cammy lives in Lexington, Massachusetts.

PETER URKOWITZ lives in Salem, Massachusetts, where he works in a college library. He was drawn into the local poetry scene after the death of a poet friend when the community came together to remember and reflect. He stayed as a spectator and soon began writing his work. He has published poems in *Meat for Tea: The Valley Review* and in *Oddball Magazine*.

CINDY VEACH is the author of *Gloved Against Blood* (CavanKerry Press), named a finalist for the 2018 Paterson Poetry Prize. Her poems have appeared in the *Academy of American Poets Poem-a-Day*, *AGNI*, *Prairie Schooner*, *Sugar House Review*, *Poet Lore*, *Michigan Quarterly Review*, *The Journal*, *Salamander* and elsewhere. Her long poem, "Witch Kitsch," won The New England Poetry Club 2018 Samuel Washington Allen Prize. She is a poetry editor for *The Mom Egg Review*.

J. MARCUS WEEKLEY, many days, dislikes being human, though he does enjoy horror movies and sci-fi. His writing is forthcoming (or newly published) in *Cake*, *The Cardiff Review*, *Inflectionist*, and *The Curator*. Weekley's collection of ekphrastic prose poems, *Singing in the Merman Cemetery*, is forthcoming in 2019 from CW Books (preorders for fifteen bucks). He also paints, photographs, and writes screenplays.

SANDY WEISMAN is a poet and visual artist. Her poetry appears in two anthologies and several journals, including *Salamander*, *Spillway*, *Barrow Street*, *Off the Coast*, and *Muddy River Poetry Review*. She is the owner of 26 Split Rock Cove, an artist community of studios, an artist living space, and workshops overlooking Mussel Ridge Channel in S. Thomaston, ME.

JULY WESTHALE is the award-winning author of *Trailer Trash* (selected for the 2016 Kore Press Book Prize), *The Cavalcade*, and *Occasionally Accurate Science*. Her most recent poetry can be found in *The National Poetry Review*, *Prairie Schooner*, *CALYX*, *Rappahannock Review*, *Tupelo Quarterly*, *RHINO*, *Lunch Ticket*, and *Quarterly West*. Her essays have been nominated for *Best American Essays* and have appeared in *McSweeney's*, *Autostraddle*, and *The Huffington Post*. She is the 2018 University of Arizona Poetry Center Fellow. www.julywesthale.com

NICOLE ZDEB is a writer in Portland, OR. She holds an MFA from Iowa Writers' Workshop and a certificate in translation from CUNY. In 2011, Bedouin Press published her chapbook, *The Friction of Distance*.